ods

Project

ollege
ndra Road West

Main authors   John Higgo
                          Paul Roder
                          David Tall
                          Thelma Wilson

                          With contributions from

                          Rajiv Bobal
                          Stan Dolan
                          Kevin Williamson

Team leaders   Paul Roder and David Tall

Project director   Stan Dolan

The authors would like to give special thanks to Ann White for her help in preparing this book for publication.

Photographs by Hugh O'Neill and Paul Roder

Cartoon by Paul Holland

Graphics by Bunny Graphics

Published by the Press Syndicate of the University of Cambridge
The Pitt Building, Trumpington Street, Cambridge CB2 1RP
40 West 20th Street, New York, NY 10011-4211, USA
10 Stamford Road, Oakleigh, Victoria 3166, Australia

First published 1992

Produced by 16-19 Mathematics, Southampton

Printed in Great Britain by Scotprint Ltd., Musselburgh.

ISBN 0 521 42648 0

Contents

1 Errors

1.1 Catastrophic errors

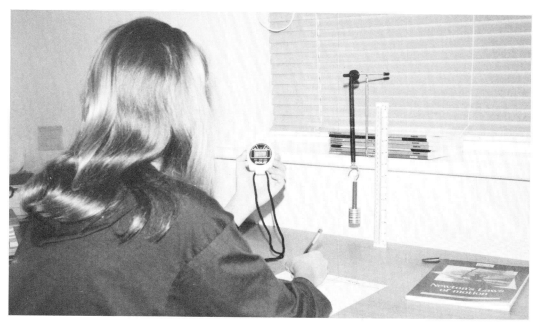

Errors occur in practical measurements as a result of:

- the inaccuracy of the instrument used for measuring;

- the accumulation of errors when calculations are performed;

- the way numbers are stored and processed by computers and calculators.

The first two of these problems have already been discussed in *Mathematical methods* and are revised in Tasksheet 1.

   TASKSHEET 1 – *The arithmetic of errors*

Errors can occur when calculating numerical derivatives in the form $\frac{f(x+h)-f(x)}{h}$ for small values of h. For example, a BBC Master computer gives:

$$\frac{\sin\left(\frac{\pi}{3}+h\right)-\sin\left(\frac{\pi}{3}\right)}{h} = 0.465661287, \text{ when } h = 0.00000001.$$

The numerical derivative tends to $\cos\left(\frac{\pi}{3}\right) = 0.5$ as h tends to zero. Clearly, the above numerical value is not very accurate.

Comparing the BBC Master and Archimedes computers, for the same calculation with different values of h, the following table of results is obtained:

h	BBC Master	Archimedes
1×10^{-1}	0.455901884	0.455901886
1×10^{-2}	0.495661539	0.495661586
1×10^{-3}	0.499954913	0.499567017
1×10^{-4}	0.499980524	0.499957241
1×10^{-5}	0.499980524	0.500003807
1×10^{-6}	0.499654561	0.500120223
1×10^{-7}	0.500585884	0.500585884
1×10^{-8}	0.465661287	0.512227416
1×10^{-9}	0.232830644	0.698491931
1×10^{-10}	0	0

They differ so much for small values of h that they cannot **both** be right!

(a) Investigate the values of $\dfrac{\sin\left(\frac{\pi}{3} + h\right) - \sin\left(\frac{\pi}{3}\right)}{h}$ for small values of h. A calculator often gives more accurate values than those shown in the table. However, the results may be strange when h is very small.

(b) Calculate $\dfrac{e^{h} - e^{0}}{h}$ for small values of h. What happens as h becomes smaller?

Catastrophic errors can also occur when a large number of calculations are performed. For example, in calculating the numerical area under a curve, if there is a specific error in calculating each strip, then using more strips may **increase** the possible error.

Suppose the area of each strip is calculated with an accuracy of 10^{-8}. Then using 100 strips gives a possible error of 100×10^{-8}. Using a million strips **increases** the possible contribution of these errors to $1\,000\,000 \times 10^{-8} = 0.01$.

Exercise 1

1. (a) The value of $\frac{2.3 \times 3.4}{1.1}$ is calculated. Assuming that each number is measured to an accuracy of ± 0.05, what is the range of values of the result?

    (b) If the accuracy is only ± 0.1 for each number, what is the range of values of the result?

2. What is the maximum possible error in calculating $\frac{3.57 - 3.22}{5.13 - 4.87}$ where each individual number is known to be accurate to ± 0.05?

3. (a) If one hundred numbers are added together, each with an error of ± 0.01, what is the possible error in the sum?

    (b) The area under a curve is calculated by adding together the area of thin strips. If a calculator makes an error of $\pm 10^{-6}$ in the area of each strip, how accurate could you guarantee the answer to be if a thousand strips are used?

4. Suppose a calculator stores results to 13 significant figure accuracy and that

    $$\sin \frac{\pi}{3} = 0.8660254037840 \quad \text{and} \quad \sin \left(\frac{\pi}{3} + 7 \times 10^{-13}\right) = 0.8660254037844,$$

    the possible error in each case being $\pm 5 \times 10^{-14}$.

    (a) Use these results to work out $\sin \left(\frac{\pi}{3} + 7 \times 10^{-13}\right) - \sin \left(\frac{\pi}{3}\right)$ in the form $a \pm e$.

    (b) Hence calculate the numerical derivative $\dfrac{\sin \left(\frac{\pi}{3} + 7 \times 10^{-13}\right) - \sin \left(\frac{\pi}{3}\right)}{7 \times 10^{-13}}$

    in the form $b \pm f$.

1.2 Bits and bytes

The memory of a calculator or computer simply consists of devices which can store a charge and be either 'on' or 'off'. Such a device can be thought of as representing a 0 or a 1. Each 0 or 1 is called a **bit** (a contraction of the words BInary digiT). For convenience, bits are grouped together eight at a time to give a **byte**, xxxxxxxx, where each x is either 0 or 1. As there are two choices for each of the eight positions, each byte can store one of $2^8 = 256$ different numbers from 00000000, 00000001, ... , to 11111111.

These bytes can be thought of as whole numbers in a **binary** (or **base two**) number system. The familiar denary number system uses ten characters (0, 1, 2, 3, ... , 9), whereas a binary number system uses just two characters (0 and 1).

The denary value of a binary number can be calculated as follows:

$$\begin{array}{cccccccc} 2^7 & 2^6 & 2^5 & 2^4 & 2^3 & 2^2 & 2^1 & 2^0 \\ 0 & 0 & 0 & 1 & 0 & 0 & 1 & 1 \end{array}$$

$00010011_2 = 1 \times 16 + 0 \times 8 + 0 \times 4 + 1 \times 2 + 1 \times 1 = 19$

(a)   **Write in denary**   (i) 00001001_2 (ii) 00101100_2

(b)   **Write in binary**   (i)   27   (ii)   15

Numbers with fractional parts can be represented as binary numbers using the binary equivalent of decimals. Extending the place values as shown:

$$\begin{array}{cccccccc} 2^3 & 2^2 & 2^1 & 2^0 & . & 2^{-1} & 2^{-2} & 2^{-3} & 2^{-4} \\ 0 & 1 & 0 & 1 & . & 0 & 0 & 1 & 1 \end{array}$$

$0101.0011_2 = 1 \times 4 + 0 \times 2 + 1 \times 1 + 0 \times \frac{1}{2} + 0 \times \frac{1}{4} + 1 \times \frac{1}{8} + 1 \times \frac{1}{16} = 5\frac{3}{16}$

Write in denary (a) 101.101_2 **(b)** 0.01011_2

To convert any decimal fraction into binary, you express it as halves, quarters, ... There is a simple procedure to do this by successive doubling. To find how many halves, double the number; if the result is bigger than one, the original is 'a half plus something'. Take the remaining 'something' and repeat the process. For example, to convert $\frac{1}{10}$ into binary:

(1)   0.1 times 2 gives 0.2, which is **0** + 0.2, giving first digit **0**,
(2)   0.2 times 2 gives 0.4, which is **0** + 0.4, giving second digit **0**,
(3)   0.4 times 2 gives 0.8, which is **0** + 0.8, giving third digit **0**,
(4)   0.8 times 2 gives 1.6, which is **1** + 0.6, giving fourth digit **1**,
(5)   0.6 times 2 gives 1.2, which is **1** + 0.2, giving fifth digit **1**,
(6)   0.2 times 2 gives 0.4, which is **...**

4

The digits now repeat from (2) onwards and so the binary representation of $\frac{1}{10}$ is

0.0 0011 0011 0011 0011 ...

If this method is performed with any rational number, then the representation will either terminate after a finite number of steps or will eventually repeat. The representation of an irrational number, such as π or $\sqrt{2}$, does not repeat.

(a) **By using repeated doubling, show that $\frac{1}{3}$ is represented in binary as 0.010101 ...**

(b) **Find the binary representation of $\frac{4}{5}$.**

(c) **Find the first ten digits of the binary expansion of π.**

You can add numbers in binary using the results $1 + 1 = 10_2$ (i.e. $1 + 1 = 2$) and $1 + 1 + 1 = 11_2$ (i.e. $1 + 1 + 1 = 3$).

Example 1

Add the following binary numbers

(a) $00111011 + 00010011_2$ (b) $00101010 + 00101010_2$

Solution

(a) 0 0 1 1 1 0 1 1
     0 0 0 1 0 0 1 1 +
     ─────────────────
     0 1 0 0 1 1 1 0
       1 1   1 1

(b) 0 0 1 0 1 0 1 0
     0 0 1 0 1 0 1 0 +
     ─────────────────
     0 1 0 1 0 1 0 0
       1   1   1

The process of subtraction in a computer is basically the same as that of addition with the subtracted number being stored as a negative number. One method of distinguishing between positive and negative numbers is to use the left-most bit to represent the **sign** of the number. A single byte can therefore represent any binary number in the range -1111111 to $+ 1111111_2$ (i.e. ± 127 in base ten).

1.3 Floating point notation

Calculators do not store decimals exactly. They usually represent numbers to a fixed number of digits. On an 8–digit calculator, π might be represented as 3.1415927. Very large and very small numbers are represented in **exponent form**. For example, 100 000 000 000 π might be written as 3.145927E11, which denotes $3.145927 \times 10^{11.}$

> **(a)** **Use a calculator to write the following numbers in exponent form to 8 significant figures.**
>
> $$100 + \sqrt{3}, \quad 1000000 + \sqrt{2}, \quad \pi^2, \quad e^{-22}.$$
>
> **(b)** **Convert to decimal: 1.2E2, 2E–3, 5.37E5.**

Numbers are stored in calculators and computers using the binary equivalent of exponent notation. For example, 96 is 1100000_2 and can be written as $0.11_2 \times 2^7$. (Writing the base, 2, and exponent, 7, in base ten is inconsistent but convenient.)

> **(a)** 0.11_2 is $\frac{1}{2} + \frac{1}{4} = \frac{3}{4}$ in base ten. Check that $\frac{3}{4} \times 2^7 = 96$.
>
> **(b)** What base ten number does $0.1011_2 \times 2^3$ represent?

This way of writing numbers is also called **floating point notation.**

> **A binary number can be written in floating point notation by expressing it in the form $a \times 2^b$.**
>
> **a is called the *mantissa* and b is called the *exponent* (or *index*). The exponent, b, is always an integer. The mantissa is always a binary fraction such that $0.1 \leq |a| < 1.0$.**

Example 2

Write the number 18 in binary using floating point notation.

Solution

$$18 = \frac{18}{32} \times 32 = \left(\frac{1}{2} + \frac{1}{16}\right) \times 2^5$$

$$= 0.1001_2 \times 2^5$$

> **Write the number 12.5 in binary using floating point notation.**

1.4   Accuracy

If a number, $a \times 2^b$, is stored in floating point notation, then the integer exponent, b, may be stored as a single byte, allowing 2^b to lie between 2^{-127} and 2^{127}. The mantissa, a, can be stored using several successive bytes, with the first bit representing the sign of a and successive bits representing the numbers of halves, quarters, eighths, etc ... For example, the number stored as shown below uses four bytes for a and one byte for b.

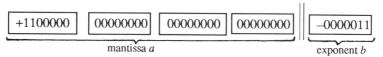

In this case, $a = \frac{3}{4}$ and $b = -3$, so the number stored is $\frac{3}{4} \times 2^{-3} = \frac{3}{32}$.

(a)   **What base ten number is stored as**

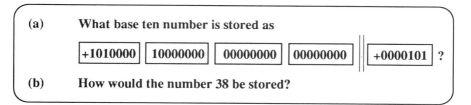

(b)   **How would the number 38 be stored?**

Not all numbers can be stored accurately. A number such as 0.6 may look exact on a calculator display, but its binary decimal

0.1001100 11001100 11001100 11001100 11001100 1 ...

does not terminate and so cannot be represented precisely in four bytes:

| +1001100 | 11001100 | 11001100 | 11001100 | 1100 ... |

error

> **The figures given on a computer or a calculator display cannot be guaranteed to be accurate.**

Errors caused by the way numbers are stored can be compounded when arithmetic operations are carried out. It can be difficult to predict errors because the software is often designed to reduce their effect. For example, more digits may be used during an arithmetic process than the standard 8 or so figures displayed at the end of the calculation.

Nevertheless, strange things may happen when:

•   adding (or subtracting) numbers of very different sizes;

•   dividing by small numbers;

•   making a large number of calculations.

After working through this chapter you should:

1. know that if measurements are added or subtracted, then the errors add;

2. know that if measurements are multiplied or divided then the approximate relative error of the result is the sum of the relative errors;

3. understand why catastrophically large errors may occur when dividing one small number by another;

4. understand the terms: binary number, binary digit, bit, byte;

5. know that numbers are often stored in floating point form as $a \times 2^b$;

6. understand why many fractions cannot be stored exactly and why the small inaccuracies can cause problems when errors are compounded through several arithmetic operations.

The arithmetic of errors

Errors in addition and subtraction

The notation $a \pm e$ (for $e > 0$) is used to denote the fact that a given measurement lies between $a - e$ and $a + e$. It is easily shown that:

> **If measurements are added or subtracted, then the errors add:**
>
> $$(a \pm e) + (b \pm f) = (a + b) \pm (e + f)$$
> $$(a \pm e) - (b \pm f) = (a - b) \pm (e + f)$$

For example, if two measurements are 11.1 ± 0.05 and 5.21 ± 0.01, then the smallest possible value of the sum is

$$11.1 - 0.05 + 5.21 - 0.01 = 16.31 - 0.06 = 16.25$$

and the largest is

$$11.1 + 0.05 + 5.21 + 0.01 = 16.31 + 0.06 = 16.37$$

The true value is in the range 16.31 ± 0.06, where ± 0.06 is obtained by adding the original errors ± 0.01 and ± 0.05.

1. Two lengths are measured as 107.5 ± 0.2 cm and 6.2 ± 0.1 cm. Find the range of values of the sum of these lengths and of the difference of these lengths.

2. The calculation $12.3 + 13.7 - 10.4$ is performed. Given that each number is only measured accurately to within ± 0.1, investigate the possible range of values of the result.

Errors in multiplication and division

When multiplying approximate numbers, it is useful to express a measurement $a \pm e$ in the form $a(1 \pm r)$ where $r = \dfrac{e}{a}$ is called the **relative error**. This concept proves useful when multiplying or dividing inaccurate measurements.

> **If measurements are multiplied or divided and the relative errors are small, then the approximate relative errors of the result is the sum of the relative errors.**
>
> $$a(1 \pm r) \times b(1 \pm s) \approx ab(1 \pm (r + s))$$
>
> $$\frac{a(1 \pm r)}{b(1 \pm s)} \approx \frac{a}{b}(1 \pm (r + s))$$

(continued)

9

For example, suppose a is measured as 3.1 ± 0.05 and b as 2.7 ± 0.05. Then the relative error of a is $\frac{0.05}{3.1} \approx 0.0161$ and that of b is $\frac{0.05}{2.7} = 0.0185$. The relative error of the product is approximately $0.0161 + 0.0185 = 0.0346$.

3.   Find the relative errors for each of the numbers 5.2 ± 0.05 and 3.7 ± 0.05 and hence calculate the relative errors of the product. Show that this estimates the product to be in the range 19.24 ± 0.44 to two decimal places. Find the maximum and minimum values of $(5.2 \pm 0.05)(3.7 \pm 0.05)$ by direct calculation and compare this to the estimated error.

4.   Find the range of values of

$$\frac{3.2 \pm 0.05}{1.3 \pm 0.05}$$

by using relative errors. Compare this with a direct calculation of the largest and smallest possible values.

5.   Use the identity $(1 + s)(1 - s) = 1 - s^2$ to show that, if r and s are small, then

$$\frac{1 + r}{1 - s} = \frac{(1 + r)(1 + s)}{1 - s^2} \approx 1 + r + s$$

If a, b, r and s are all positive and r and s are small, show that

$$\frac{a(1 \pm r)}{b(1 \pm s)} \text{ lies between } \frac{a(1 - r)}{b(1 + s)} \text{ and } \frac{a(1 + r)}{b(1 - s)}$$

Deduce the relative error rule

$$\frac{a(1 \pm r)}{b(1 \pm s)} \approx \frac{a}{b}(1 \pm (r + s))$$

Tutorial sheet

1.   A hundred numbers are added together, each with an error of ± 0.05. What is the possible range of error in the sum? In calculating the area under a curve using the sum of the area of strips, will the calculation necessarily improve in accuracy by taking a very large number of strips?

2.   A ball rolls a distance 5.65 metres in 3.2 seconds. The distance is measured to ± 0.05 metres and the time to ± 0.1 second. Calculate the relative error of each measurement and hence estimate the range of values for the speed in metres per second.

3.   Using the doubling process, convert the following decimal fractions to binary fractions:

   (a)   0.75   (b)   0.6   (c) $\frac{3}{7}$ (d) $\frac{2}{3}$

4.   Express e in binary using floating point notation. (Write the mantissa to 10 binary places.)

5.   Which of the following numbers will terminate, which will repeat, and which will continue without a repeating pattern, when converted to binary expansions?

   (a) $\frac{7}{8}$ (b)   0.0625   (c)   0.8   (d) $\frac{2}{9}$ (e) $\frac{1}{\sqrt{2}}$

6.   Which of the following sums do you think will give exactly 100 on a computer or calculator?

   (a) $1 + 1 + \ldots + 1$ (100 terms)
   (b) $0.5 + 0.5 + \ldots + 0.5$ (200 terms)
   (c) $0.1 + 0.1 + \ldots + 0.1$ (1000 terms)
   (d) $0.0625 + 0.0625 + \ldots + 0.0625$ (1600 terms)

7.   Imagine a very simple calculating device which stores binary numbers by first changing them to floating point form, $a \times 2^{b}$. Suppose further that it uses just one byte for each number with the first half byte being used for the binary fraction, a, and the second half for the exponent, b

$$\boxed{\pm}\boxed{* \ * \ *}\boxed{\pm}\boxed{* \ * \ *}$$
$$\quad\quad a \quad\quad\quad\quad b$$

As one bit is used for the sign, the device can only store the three most significant binary digits in a.

   (a)   Show how the device would store these numbers in a single byte.
      (i)   0.000101   (ii)   10.101   (iii)   0.0101101

   (b)   If $A = \boxed{+}\boxed{1 \ 1 \ 0}\boxed{-}\boxed{0 \ 0 \ 1}$ and $B = \boxed{+}\boxed{1 \ 0 \ 0}\boxed{+}\boxed{0 \ 0 \ 1}$

      show how the device would store,   (i) $A + A$ (ii) $A + B$

   (c)   Explain why, for this device, $(A + A) + B \neq (A + B) + A$.

11

2 Areas

2.1 Rules for estimating areas under graphs

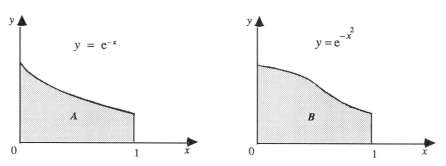

You can use algebraic integration to find area *A* shown above, but you would need to use a numerical method to find area *B*.

Four rules which you can use to find areas numerically are as follows:

(i)   First ordinate rule   (ii)   Last ordinate rule

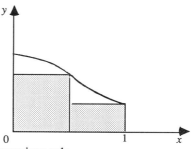

(iii)   Mid-ordinate rule   (iv)   Trapezium rule

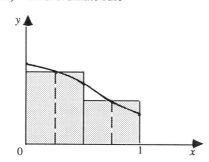
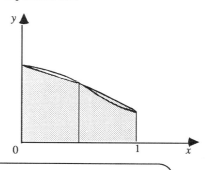

Estimate $\displaystyle\int_{0}^{1} e^{-x^2}\, \mathrm{d}x$ by each of the rules above using two strips each time.

 TASKSHEET 1 - *Accuracy*

12

From your answers to Tasksheet 1 you should see that:

- for the first and last ordinate rules, doubling the number of strips (so halving the width of the strips) approximately halves the error; dividing the width of the strips by three approximately divides the error by three, and so on;

- for the mid-ordinate and trapezium rules, halving the width of the strips approximately divides the error by 2^2 or 4; dividing the width of the strips by 3 approximately divides the error by 3^2 or 9, and so on.

> For small h, if the error changes by a factor λ^n when the strip width, h, is changed by a factor λ, then the method is said to be an *approximation with order of accuracy n* or an *nth order approximation*.
>
> - The first and last ordinate rules are first order approximations .
>
> - The trapezium and mid-ordinate rules are second order approximations.

A **second order** method is better than a **first order** method because the error decreases faster as the number of strips is increased.

> (a)   Describe what will happen as the strip width changes for a rule which gives a third order approximation.
>
> (b)   The first and last ordinate rules (both first order approximations) give exact answers for constant functions but not for polynomials of degree 1 or more. For what degree of polynomial do the trapezium and mid-ordinate rules stop being exact?

If you take the mean of the first and last ordinate rules, you obtain the more accurate trapezium rule. It is worth investigating whether an average of the trapezium and mid-ordinate rules also results in a new rule of higher order.

> You should have noticed that the errors for the trapezium rule and the mid-ordinate rule were not the same. By looking at the respective errors, suggest a *weighted average* of the formulas for the two rules which it would be sensible to try.
>
> Use your data from Tasksheet 1 to investigate the error of the answers given by this weighted average as you increase the number of strips. What is the order of approximation of this new rule?

2.2   Simpson's rule

The weighted average

$$\frac{(2 \times \text{mid-ordinate rule answer}) + (\text{trapezium rule answer})}{3}$$

is called Simpson's rule, after Thomas Simpson (1710-1761). Simpson did not have a University education. He was a weaver by trade, but became a professor of mathematics and fellow of the Royal Society. He published work on the laws of chance, algebra, geometry and trigonometry and contributed to the development of the Newton-Raphson method of solving equations

In the previous section you found that Simpson's Rule was a fourth order approximation, since doubling the number of strips caused the error to be divided by 2^4.

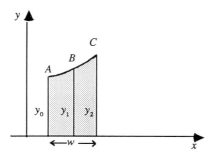

For the area of the shaded region, the mid-ordinate rule gives wy_1 and the trapezium rule gives $\frac{1}{2}w\,(y_0 + y_2)$

Simpson's rule therefore estimates the area as

$$\frac{2wy_1 + \frac{1}{2}w\,(y_0 + y_2)}{3} = \frac{1}{6}\,w\,(y_0 + 4y_1 + y_2)$$

It is conventional to describe the above formula as being Simpson's rule for **two** strips. Let the width of each strip be h (so $w = 2h$).

The formula then simplifies to

$$\frac{1}{3}h\,(y_0 + 4y_1 + y_2)$$

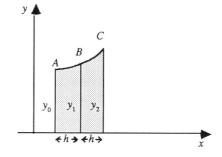

Simpson's rule for two strips estimates the area as
$$\frac{1}{3}\,h\,(y_0 + 4y_1 + y_2)$$
This is an approximation of order 4.

For the four strips below, Simpson's rule would give:

$$\frac{1}{3}h\,(y_0 + 4y_1 + y_2) + \frac{1}{3}h\,(y_2 + 4y_3 + y_4)$$

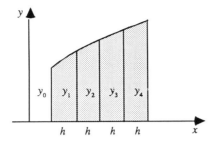 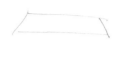

> **Use Simpson's rule with four strips to estimate** $\displaystyle\int_0^2 \cos x\,dx$.

By comparing the accuracy of your last answer with those obtained in Tasksheet 1 from the trapezium and mid-ordinate rules, you should see why Simpson's rule was so useful in pre-calculator days. This might not seem so important now that computers can be used for calculation, but the small number of strips needed reduces rounding errors of the sort discussed in Chapter 1. For this reason, Simpson's rule is used for built-in area functions in some scientific calculators.

The formula for Simpson's rule with four strips can be simplified to give:

$$\frac{1}{3}h\,(y_0 + 4y_1 + 2y_2 + 4y_3 + y_4) = \frac{1}{3}h\,(y_0 + y_4 + 4\,(y_1 + y_3) + 2y_2)$$

The general formula for Simpson's rule with n strips, n even, is:

$$\frac{1}{3}h\,[y_0 + y_n + 4\,(y_1 + y_3 + \ldots + y_{n-1}) + 2\,(y_2 + y_4 + \ldots + y_{n-2})]$$

> (a)   Check that putting $n = 4$ gives the formula for four strips.
>
> (b)   Write down the formula for Simpson's rule with eight strips.
>
> (c)   For Simpson's rule with n strips , explain why n must be even.

15

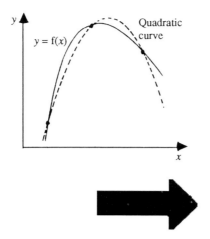

Quadratic curve

$y = f(x)$

Simpson derived his rule by a method quite different to the one used here. He joined sets of three points on the curve with quadratic curves. The diagram shows why this is likely to lead to an accurate estimate. Simpson's method is considered in detail on Tasksheet 2.

TASKSHEET 2 - *Simpson's rule*

You will need a program for Simpson's rule for the following exercise. Try to write one by adapting your trapezium rule program. An appropriate program is given in the unit guide.

Exercise 1

1. It is not possible to evaluate $\int_{0}^{1.5} \sin x^2 \, dx$ by algebraic integration.

   Estimate the area using Simpson's rule. How many strips do you need to use to be sure of having an answer correct to 4 significant figures?

2. Use Simpson's rule to evaluate $\int_{0}^{2} \frac{1}{x^2 + 4} \, dx$ correct to 7 d.p.

3. A pillar is built up from two sections, each of height 6 metres. For each section the radius (r metres) at a height h metres above the base is as shown:

h	0	1.5	3	4.5	6
r	2	1.8	1.5	1.8	2

   Estimate the volume of the pillar.

4. (a) Evaluate $\displaystyle\int_1^2 (3x^2 + 4x + 3)\, dx$ exactly, using algebraic integration.

    (b) Estimate $\displaystyle\int_1^2 (3x^2 + 4x + 3)\, dx$ using Simpson's rule for two strips.
    What do you notice?

5. Choose any cubic function, f(x). Evaluate $\displaystyle\int_1^2 f(x)\, dx$ exactly and then use
    Simpson's rule with two strips. Repeat the procedure for a different function or
    for different limits. What do you notice?

6E. If you have studied the unit *The Normal distribution*, you will have met the
    function

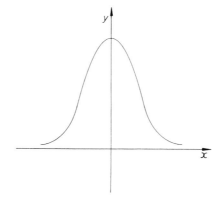

    Use Simpson's rule to check that the total area underneath the graph of this
    function is equal to 1. Also, check some of the entries in the Normal probability
    tables.

2.3 Simpson's rule and cubic functions

You have seen that Simpson's rule appears to give an exact answer, with any number of strips, for cubic as well as quadratic functions.

It is quite easy to see why this is the case for strips symmetrically placed about $x = 0$ if the cubic graph is that of $y = x^3$.

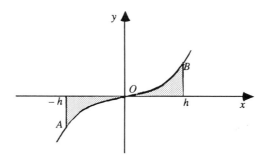

By symmetry, the exact value of $\int_{-h}^{h} x^3 \, dx$ is zero.

The value given by Simpson's rule with two strips is

$$\tfrac{1}{3} h \left[(-h)^3 + 4 \times 0^3 + (h)^3 \right],$$

which is also zero.

Another interesting way to see that Simpson's rule will be exact in this case is to use the fact that Simpson's rule gives the exact area under a quadratic through A, O and B. In this case the quadratic is simply a straight line.

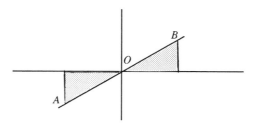

> **Find the equation of this straight line approximation to $y = x^3$.**

The work above has only proved that Simpson's rule is exact for the particular cubic $y = x^3$, when the strips are symmetrically placed about $x = 0$. Tasksheet 3E generalises this result.

TASKSHEET 3E - *Cubics*

18

You have seen that the first and last ordinate rules, which are first order approximations, are only exact for polynomials of degree 0 and that the trapezium and mid-ordinate rules, which are second order approximations, are exact for polynomials of degree 0 and 1.

> **Simpson's rule is a fourth order approximation. For what degree of polynomial is it exact? What appears to be the connection between the order of approximation and the degree of polynomial for which a rule is exact?**

This connection between orders of approximation and degrees of polynomials will be considered further in the chapter on Taylor polynomials.

After working through this chapter you should:

1. be able to estimate areas using first ordinate, last ordinate, mid-ordinate, trapezium and Simpson's rules;

2. know that the order of approximation of the first and last ordinate rules is 1, of the trapezium and mid-ordinate rules is 2 and of Simpson's rule is 4;

3. appreciate that Simpson's rule will nearly always give a very accurate answer even for a small number of strips, but that problems will arise near discontinuities.

Accuracy

1. It is clear that $\int_0^1 e^{-x^2} dx$ is between the answers given by the first ordinate and last ordinate rules. For what functions do the first and last ordinate rules both give an exact answer?

2. For $\int_0^1 e^{-x^2} dx$, the trapezium rule gives an answer smaller than the area required and the mid-ordinate rule gives too large an answer.

   (a) What happens if you use these two rules for $\int_0^1 e^{-x} dx$?

   (b) For what functions will the mid-ordinate and trapezium rules both give an exact answer ?

   (c) Use a diagram to help you explain how, for any function, you can work out the trapezium rule answer from the answers given by the first and last ordinate rules.

It may seem pointless to use a numerical method for an integral which can be evaluated with complete accuracy by algebraic methods, but doing so will enable you to analyse the error arising from the use of numerical methods. For example:

You know that $\int_0^2 x^4 dx = \left[\dfrac{x^5}{5} \right]_0^2 = 6.4$. Using the first ordinate rule with 10 strips gives

4.907 (to 4 s.f.), so the error is -1.493. Increasing the number of strips to 20 gives the integral as 5.627 (to 4 s.f.) so the error is -0.773.

In questions 3 and 4, you should use programs for the four rules and, to save time, you can work with another student if you wish. Appropriate programs are given in the unit guide.

3. Copy and complete this table for estimates of $\int_0^2 x^4 dx$ using the four numerical rules.

   For the first and last ordinate rules, answers to 3 decimal places are sufficient, but it will be helpful for later work if you give the other answers to 8 decimal places.

No. of strips	First ordinate		Last ordinate		Mid-ordinate		Trapezium	
	Area	Error	Area	Error	Area	Error	Area	Error
10	4.907	– 1.493						
20								
30								
40								

4. Repeat question 3, replacing x^4 in the integral by: (a) x^5 (b) $\cos x$ (c) e^x.

5. Write a clear account describing what effect increasing the number of strips by a given factor has on the error for each of the four rules.

Simpson's rule

Simpson's rule gives:

$$\frac{1}{3} h (y_0 + 4y_1 + y_2)$$
as an approximation to
the shaded area opposite.

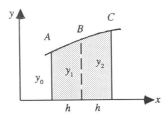

It is always possible to draw a quadratic curve through three points. (If the three points are in a straight line, the quadratic equation has the form $y = 0x^2 + bx + c$.)

Simpson derived his formula by considering a quadratic curve through three points on a curve with equally spaced x-coordinates, such as A, B and C above.

In this tasksheet you will see that the integral of this quadratic function gives the Simpson's rule formula.

Start by choosing the three points with B on the y-axis.

Let the quadratic curve through A, B and C have equation $y = ax^2 + bx + c$, where a, b and c are constants.

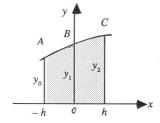

1.   Let $I = \displaystyle\int_{-h}^{h} (ax^2 + bx + c)\,dx$. Show that $I = \frac{2}{3} ah^3 + 2ch$

Questions 2 and 3 show that $\frac{1}{3} h (y_0 + 4y_1 + y_2)$ is equal to I.

2.   Since point A lies on the curve $y = ax^2 + bx + c$,

$$y_0 = a(-h)^2 + b(-h) + c$$
$$= ah^2 - bh + c.$$

Write down the corresponding equations for y_1 and y_2.

3.   Use the results of question 2 to show that $\frac{1}{3} h (y_0 + 4y_1 + y_2)$ is equal to I.

The work above shows the derivation of Simpson's rule for two strips which are symmetrically placed around $x = 0$.

By translating the curve, the strips could be in any position and so the derivation holds for any such strips.

21

Cubics

Consider the general cubic:
$y = ax^3 + bx^2 + cx + d$.

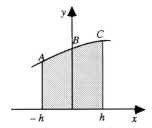

First consider a strip symmetrically placed about $x = 0$. If Simpson's rule is to be exact, the shaded area must be exactly the same as the area under the quadratic curve on which A, B and C lie.

1.　　Since A lies on $y = ax^3 + bx^2 + cx + d$, it follows that its coordinates are $(-h, -ah^3 + bh^2 - ch + d)$. Write down the coordinates of B and C.

2.　　Let the equation of the quadratic curve through A, B and C be
$$y = px^2 + qx + r.$$

Since A lies on the quadratic
$$ph^2 - qh + r = -ah^3 + bh^2 - ch + d.$$

Write down the equivalent equations for B and C.

3.　　Using the equations from question 2, show that the quadratic through A, B and C has equation
$$y = bx^2 + (ah^2 + c)x + d.$$

4.　　For Simpson's rule to be exact it is necessary to show that
$$\int_{-h}^{h} (ax^3 + bx^2 + cx + d)\, dx = \int_{-h}^{h} (bx^2 + (ah^2 + c)x + d)\, dx$$

Complete the proof that Simpson's rule is exact for the symmetrically placed strip.

The work above shows that Simpson's rule is exact for cubics if the strips are symmetrically placed around $x = 0$. If the strips are placed elsewhere then the graph can be translated as shown below.

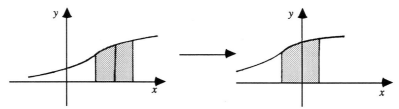

This translations does not change the area underneath the graph, nor does it change the Simpson's rule estimate. Simpson's rule is therefore exact for any cubic graph.

22

Tutorial sheet

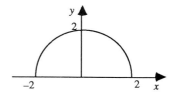

You may remember that, in *Introductory calculus*, you used the trapezium rule to estimate the area of a circle of radius 2 units.

The semi-circle shown above, with radius 2 and centre the origin, has the equation $y = \sqrt{(4 - x^2)}$.

The area of the semi-circle is $\frac{1}{2} \pi \times 2^2 = 2\pi$, and so

$$\int_0^2 \sqrt{(4 - x^2)} \, dx = \pi.$$

An estimate for π can therefore be obtained by using numerical integration for $\int_0^2 \sqrt{(4 - x^2)} \, dx$.

1. Work out the difference between the value of π given by your calculator and the values obtained by estimating $\int_0^2 \sqrt{(4 - x^2)} \, dx$ using the trapezium rule and Simpson's rule with different numbers of strips. Tabulate your answers.

2.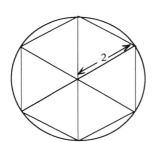

There is a method unconnected with calculus which enables the area π to be estimated.

The diagram shows a circle of radius 2 units containing a regular hexagon split into 6 equilateral triangles.

(a) Using the fact that $1\frac{1}{2}$ triangles fit inside a quarter circle, explain why $3 \sin 60° < \pi$.

(b) Sketch a regular octagon inside a circle and use the sketch to explain why $4 \sin 45° < \pi$.

(c) Looking at the expressions in questions (a) and (b), write down the inequality you would expect to obtain from drawing a regular 12-sided polygon inside a circle.

Write down the inequality for an *n*-sided polygon.

(continued)

3. It is clear that the inequalities of question 2 give increasingly accurate estimates for π. Write a simple program to investigate the accuracy of these estimates as you increase the number of sides of the polygon.

    Discuss the relative accuracy of this method, the trapezium rule and Simpson's rule, relative to the number of divisions of the quarter circle which are used.

4. The circle is one shape for which Simpson's rule does not quickly give very accurate answers. What do you think is the property of a graph of a quarter circle that makes Simpson's rule less accurate?

5. (a) Investigate what happens when you try to integrate $y = \dfrac{1}{\cos x}$, $y = \dfrac{1}{\sin x}$ and $y = \dfrac{1}{\tan x}$, for $0.000001 \leq x \leq 1$ using Simpson's rule. Try to explain why you do not get consistent answers for two of the three areas.

    (b) Why was the range $0 \leq x \leq 1$ not used in part (a)?

6. Investigate the use of Simpson's rule for areas near $x = 0$ under the graphs of $y = x^{1/2}$ and $y = x^{-2}$. (You might like to look at the areas from $x = 0.1$ to $x = 1$, then from $x = 0.01$ to $x = 1$ and so on.) Try to explain the pattern of your answers.

3 *Taylor polynomials*

3.1 Quadratic approximations

Brook Taylor (1685-1731), was educated at home and then at St. John's College, Cambridge. He was one of England's most brilliant mathematicians and in 1715 published his *Methodus Incrementorum Directa et Inversa*, which includes the work on which this chapter is based. (In the 18th century such books were written in Latin so that they could be read throughout Europe.) Taylor was also a talented musician and artist and wrote works on perspective.

In *Introductory calculus* you used the idea that:

$$f'(a) \approx \frac{f(a+h) - f(a)}{h}$$

Re-arranging this formula gives:

$$f(a+h) \approx f(a) + f'(a)h$$

This is known as Taylor's first approximation to f(x), centred on $x = a$.

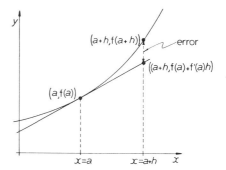

To use the approximation, you must already know the value of the function and its derivative when $x = a$. You can then estimate the value of the function for x close to a. You can, for example, easily calculate that $2^{-1} = 0.5$. Taylor's first approximation then enables you to estimate 2.08^{-1}.

Example 1

Find Taylor's first approximation to the function $f(x) = x^{-1}$ at the point where $x = 2$. Hence estimate 2.08^{-1}.

Solution

$$f(x) = x^{-1} \Rightarrow f'(x) = -x^{-2} \text{ so } f(2) = \frac{1}{2} \text{ and } f'(2) = -\frac{1}{4}$$

$$f(2+h) \approx f(2) + f'(2)h \Rightarrow (2+h)^{-1} \approx \frac{1}{2} - \frac{h}{4}$$

$$\Rightarrow (2+0.08)^{-1} \approx \frac{1}{2} - \frac{0.08}{4}$$

$$\Rightarrow 2.08^{-1} \approx 0.48$$

(a) In the example, explain why $h = x - 2$ and hence why
$$x^{-1} \approx \frac{1}{2} - \frac{(x-2)}{4}$$

(b) Use a graph plotter to superimpose the graphs of $y = x^{-1}$ and $y = \frac{1}{2} - \frac{(x-2)}{4}$ for $1.5 < x < 2.5$ and $0.4 < y < 0.6$.

You may recall from the unit *Mathematical methods* that the method of approximating a graph with a straight line was also used for solving differential equations by the step-by-step method. How good Taylor's first approximation is depends on the local straightness of the graph at the point where $x = a$. The approximation will be good over only a short interval if the graph is very curved at the point. It would therefore seem a logical next step to approximate the function with a quadratic curve.

Let $g(a + h) = p + qh + rh^2$ be a quadratic approximation to $f(a + h)$ at the point where $x = a$ (i.e. a is constant and h is a variable).

$x = a + h$ and so $h = x - a$.

Then $g(x) = p + q(x - a) + r(x - a)^2$

$\Rightarrow g'(x) = q + 2r(x - a)$

$\Rightarrow g''(x) = 2r$

Thus $g(a) = p$, $g'(a) = q$ and $g''(a) = 2r$

so $g(a + h) = g(a) + g'(a)h + g''(a)\dfrac{h^2}{2}$

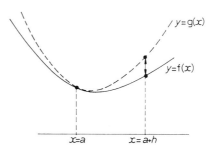

(a)   Explain why $f(a) + f'(a)h + f''(a)\dfrac{h^2}{2}$ is likely to be a good approximation to $f(a + h)$ for small values of h.

(b)   Explain why $(2 + h)^{-1} \approx \dfrac{1}{2} - \dfrac{h}{4} + \dfrac{h^2}{8}$ for small values of h.

(c)   Graph $y = x^{-1}$ and $y = \dfrac{1}{2} - \dfrac{(x-2)}{4} + \dfrac{(x-2)^2}{8}$ on the same axes.

(d)   Explain why $\ln(1 + h) \approx h - \dfrac{h^2}{2}$ for small values of h.

(e)   Rewrite the approximation given in (d) in terms of x and y and check your answer on a graph plotter.

A quadratic approximation calculated in this way is called Taylor's second approximation. It follows the graph of the function better than Taylor's first approximation because it takes into account the rate at which the gradient is changing.

Taylor's second approximation to a function $f(x)$ at $x = a$ is

$$f(a + h) \approx f(a) + f'(a)\, h + f''(a)\dfrac{h^2}{2}$$

The approximation is good for small values of h.

3.2 Estimating gradients numerically

You have seen how Taylor's first approximation to a function is a simple rearrangement of a formula for calculating the numerical derivative of the function at the point where $x = a$.

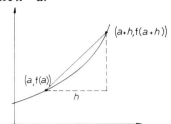

The gradient of the graph of f(x) at the point $(a, f(a))$ can be estimated by evaluating the gradient of the chord joining the points $(a, f(a))$ and $(a + h, f(a + h))$.

$$f'(a) \approx \frac{f(a + h) - f(a)}{h} \qquad ①$$

> **Use formula ① to estimate the gradient of the graph of $2^{\cos x}$ at the point where $x = 1$. Write down the answers you get for $h = 0.1, 0.01, 0.001$ and so on until you are sure that you have the answer correct to 4 s.f.**

You can also use Taylor's second approximation to find the derivative of a function.

Using Taylor's second approximation:

$$f(a + h) \approx f(a) + f'(a)\, h + f''(a)\, \frac{h^2}{2}$$

Putting $-h$ instead of h gives

$$f(a - h) \approx f(a) - f'(a)h + f''(a)\, \frac{h^2}{2}$$

So $f(a + h) - f(a - h) \approx f(a) + f'(a)h + f''(a)\, \frac{h^2}{2} - \left(f(a) - f'(a)h + f''(a)\, \frac{h^2}{2} \right)$

> **Show that this formula rearranges to give:**
> $$f'(a) \approx \frac{f(a + h) - f(a - h)}{2h}$$

The gradient of the graph of f(x) at the point $(a, f(a))$ can therefore be estimated by evaluating the gradient of the chord joining the points $(a - h, f(a - h))$ and $(a + h, f(a + h))$

$$f'(a) \approx \frac{f(a + h) - f(a - h)}{2h} \qquad ②$$

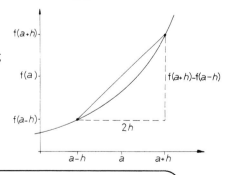

> **Use formula ② to estimate the gradient of the graph of $2^{\cos x}$ at the point where $x = 1$, using $h = 0.1, 0.01$ and so on. Compare your answers with those obtained by using formula ① .**

It is very easy to find the derivative of an elementary function such as $f(x) = \sin x$. Using a numerical method with such a function does, however, enable you to analyse the accuracy of the method.

The gradient of the graph of $y = \sin x$ at $x = 2$ is $\cos 2$.

Estimating the gradient using formula ① with $h = 0.01$ gives an error of

$$\frac{(\sin 2.01 - \sin 2)}{0.01} - \cos 2 \quad \text{, which is} -0.00454 \text{ to 3 s.f.}$$

So the error is 0.00454 to 3 s.f. (Error is defined as an absolute value.)

(a) **Copy and complete the table below:**

Errors when using formula ①

	$h = 0.01$	$h = 0.002$	$h = 0.001$
$y = \sin x$ at $x = 2$	0.00454		
$y = \sin x$ at $x = 1$			
$y = e^x$ at $x = 1$			

(b) **What happens to the error when the value of h is divided by 5 and when it is divided by 10?**

(c) **What does the order of accuracy of this method appear to be?**

(d) **Complete another table, similar to the one shown above, using formula ②.**

(e) **What does the order of accuracy of this method appear to be?**

Numerical methods for finding the derivative:

$$f'(a) \approx \frac{f(a+h) - f(a)}{h} \quad \text{is a first order approximation.}$$

$$f'(a) \approx \frac{f(a+h) - f(a-h)}{2h} \quad \text{is a second order approximation.}$$

3.3   Higher degree Taylor polynomials

Taylor's first and second approximations are both polynomials. In fact, all Taylor's approximations are polynomials with Taylor's rth approximation being a polynomial of degree r. If a function can be differentiated r times then you can fit a Taylor polynomial to it by equating the first, second, third, ... , rth derivatives of the function to those of the polynomial. The historical importance of Taylor polynomials was that they enabled tables of values of functions to be built up with great accuracy. (It is worth thinking how lengthy this process must have been with no calculators for the 'number crunching'.)

Those approximations centred on $x = 0$ (i.e. $a = 0$ in the formula) are of special interest since h is then the horizontal distance from the origin and can therefore be replaced by x.

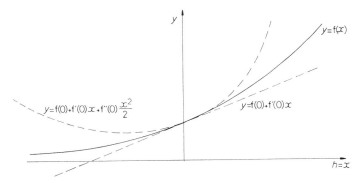

Taylor's first and second approximations centred on $x = 0$ are:
$$f(x) \approx f(0) + f'(0)x$$
and
$$f(x) \approx f(0) + f'(0)x + f''(0)\,\frac{x^2}{2}$$

Example 2

Derive Taylor's second approximation, centred on $x = 0$, for $(1 + x)^n$.

Solution

$f(x) = (1 + x)^n \Rightarrow f(0) = 1$

$f'(x) = n(1 + x)^{n-1} \Rightarrow f'(0) = n$

$f''(x) = n(n - 1)(1 + x)^{n-2} \Rightarrow f''(0) = n(n - 1)$

Substituting in $f(x) \approx f(0) + f'(0)x + f''(0)\,\frac{x^2}{2}$ gives:

$(1 + x)^n \approx 1 + nx + \frac{n(n-1)}{2}x^2$

$1 + nx + \frac{n(n-1)}{2}x^2$ was the start of the series for $(1 + x)^n$ obtained by using the binomial theorem in *Mathematical methods*. It is encouraging that the two methods give the same result!

> **What is Taylor's second approximation to f(x) = e^x centred on $x = 0$?**

Taylor's third approximation is a cubic polynomial which has the same y-coordinate and the same first, second and third derivatives as the graph of the function at the point where $x = 0$.

Let g(x) $= p + qx + rx^2 + sx^3$ then g(0) $= p$

$$g'(x) = q + 2rx + 3sx^2 \quad \Rightarrow g'(0) = q$$

But g(0) = f(0) and g$'$(0) = f$'$(0) so p = f(0) and q = f$'$(0)

(a) Work out f$''$(0) and f$^{(3)}$(0) and so find expressions for r and s.

(b) Explain how the answers above give, for Taylor's third approximation:

$$f(x) \approx f(0) + f\,'(0)x + f\,''(0)\,\frac{x^2}{2!} + f^{(3)}(0)\,\frac{x^3}{3!}$$

(c) Write down Taylor's third approximation to f(x) = e^x centred on $x = 0$.

You should now realise how to find Taylor's fourth, fifth, sixth, ... approximations centred on the point where $x = 0$.

(a) Work out Taylor's fourth approximation by starting with:

$$f(x) \approx g(x) \text{ where } g(x) = p + qx + rx^2 + sx^3 + tx^4$$

(b) Write down Taylor's fifth approximation centred on $x = 0$.

(c) Write down Taylor's fifth approximation to f(x) = e^x centred on $x = 0$.

Taylor approximations centred on $x = 0$ are often referred to as Maclaurin approximations. (You may have met these in the unit *Calculus methods*.)

Taylor's rth approximation centred on the point where $x = 0$ is

$$f(x) \approx f(0) + f'(0)x + f''(0)\frac{x^2}{2!} + \dots + f^{(r)}(0)\frac{x^r}{r!}$$

Taylor's rth approximation centred on the point where $x = a$ is

$$f(a + h) \approx f(a) + f'(a)h + f''(a)\frac{h^2}{2!} + \dots + f^{(r)}(a)\frac{h^r}{r!}$$

Although Taylor's rth approximation is a polynomial of degree r and will generally have $r + 1$ terms, you will find that terms sometimes have zero coefficients. This means that, when zero terms are not written in, a fifth approximation, for example, may have only 4 (or fewer) terms.

> **Show that Taylor's seventh approximation to $f(x) = \sin x$ centred on $x = 0$ is**
>
> $$\sin x \approx x - \frac{x^3}{3!} + \frac{x^5}{5!} - \frac{x^7}{7!}$$

Exercise 1

In this exercise all Taylor series can be taken to be centred on $x = 0$.

1. (a) Work out Taylor's fourth approximation to $(1 + x)^n$.

    (b) Derive Taylor's fourth approximation for $\frac{1}{1+x}$ by putting $n = -1$ in the polynomial for $(1 + x)^n$.

    (c) Derive Taylor's fourth approximation for $\frac{1}{1-x}$ by replacing x by $-x$ in the answer to (b).

    (d) $1 + x + x^2 + x^3 + x^4 + \dots$ is a geometrical progression. Find the sum to infinity of this series and explain the connection with (c). Find a similar connection with a geometrical progression for (b).

2. Write $\sqrt{(1 + x)}$ in the form $(1 + x)^n$.

    Hence write down and simplify Taylor's fifth approximation for $\sqrt{(1 + x)}$.

    Check the accuracy of the approximation for $x = 0.21$.

3. Taylor's fifth approximation for $\sin x$ is $x - \dfrac{x^3}{3!} + \dfrac{x^5}{5!}$.

Use this result to write down Taylor's fifth approximation for:

(a) $\sin 2x$ (b) $\sin 0.5x$.

Simplify your answers.

4. (a) By considering the graph of $\ln x$ and the derivative of $\ln x$, explain why it would not be possible to find Taylor polynomials, based on $x = 0$, for $\ln x$.

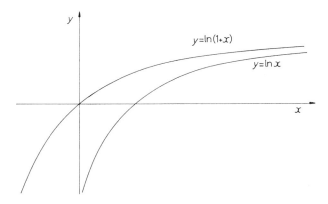

(b) Explain why it would be possible to find polynomials for $\ln (1 + x)$ and work out Taylor's second approximation for $\ln (1 + x)$.

(c) Use your answer to (b) to write down and simplify Taylor's second approximation for $\ln (1 + 0.2x)$.

3.4 Radius of convergence

Taylor's approximation centred on $x = 0$ is good for 'small' values of x, but how small is 'small'?

You know that $S_r = 1 + x + x^2 + x^3 + x^4 + \ldots + x^r$ is Taylor's rth approximation to $\dfrac{1}{1-x}$.

The table shows values of S_r for different values of x and r.

r \ x	−1.2	−1	−0.8	−0.6	−0.4	−0.2	0	0.2	0.4	0.6	0.8	1	1.2
0	1	1	1	1	1	1	1	1	1	1	1	1	1
1	−0.2	0	0.2	0.4	0.6	0.8	1	1.2	1.4	1.6	1.8	2	2.2
2	1.24	1	0.84	0.76	0.76	0.84	1	1.24	1.56	1.96	2.44	3	3.64
3	−0.488	0	0.328	0.544	0.696	0.832	1	1.248	1.624	2.176	2.952	4	5.368
4	1.5856	1	0.7376	0.674	0.7216	0.8336	1	1.2496	1.6496	2.3056	3.3616	5	7.442
5	−0.9027	0	0.4099	0.596	0.7114	0.8333	1	1.2499	1.6598	2.3834	3.6893	6	9.93
6	2.0833	1	0.6721	0.642	0.7155	0.8333	1	1.25	1.6639	2.43	3.9514	7	12.92
7	−1.4999	0	0.4623	0.615	0.7138	0.8333	1	1.25	1.6656	2.458	4.1611	8	16.5
8	2.7999	1	0.6301	0.631	0.7145	0.8333	1	1.25	1.6662	2.4748	4.3289	9	20.8
9	−2.3599	0	0.4959	0.621	0.7142	0.8333	1	1.25	1.6665	2.4849	4.4631	10	25.96
10	3.8319	1	0.6033	0.627	0.7143	0.8333	1	1.25	1.6666	2.4909	4.5705	11	32.15
11	−3.5982	0	0.5174	0.624	0.7143	0.8333	1	1.25	1.6666	2.4946	4.6564	12	39.58
12	5.3179	1	0.5861	0.626	0.7143	0.8333	1	1.25	1.6667	2.4967	4.7251	13	48.5
$\dfrac{1}{1-x}$	0.4545	0.5	0.5556	0.625	0.7143	0.8333	1	1.25	1.6667	2.5	5	∞	−5

When $x = 0.6$, the actual value of $\dfrac{1}{1-x}$ is 2.5.

Taylor's second approximation gives 1.96 which is not particularly good. Taylor's twelfth approximation, however, gives 2.4967 which is accurate to 2 decimal places.

> **Write a short program for a graphic calculator or a computer to calculate and display S_r for values of r increasing in steps of 1 from $r = 0$ when $x = 0.6$. For what value of r does Taylor's rth approximation give an accurate value when rounded to 4 decimal places?**

When you use a graphic calculator to calculate values of S_r you can also plot the graph of (r, S_r) to get a visual image of how increasing the degree of the approximation produces a sequence of results which converge on the correct value of the function.

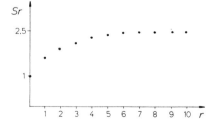

> **(a)** For which values of x does Taylor's approximation appear to converge on the correct value of the function?
>
> **(b)** Explain why the approximation is of no use for $|x| \geq 1$.

The series $S_r = 1 + x + x^2 + x^3 + x^4 + \ldots$, if summed to infinity, will converge to the value of $f(x) = \frac{1}{1-x}$ if $-1 < x < 1$.

The range $-1 < x < 1$ is called the **radius of convergence.**

If the series is summed to infinity for a value of x within the radius of convergence then there is no error i.e. **the series and the function are equal.** When the series is summed to infinity it is no longer an approximation and is called a **Taylor series** .

$$\frac{1}{1-x} = 1 + x + x^2 + x^3 + x^4 + \ldots , \text{ for } -1 < x < 1$$

The three dots at the end of the series is a conventional way of signifying that the series is summed to infinity. The tasksheet will investigate the radius of convergence for other Taylor series.

 TASKSHEET 1 – *Investigating radius of convergence*

Although it is beyond the scope of this unit to prove convergence for any series other than simple geometrical progressions, you can use short 'number crunching' programs and graph plotters to investigate the radius of convergence of a Taylor series. The following results can be proved.

$\sin x = x - \dfrac{x^3}{3!} + \dfrac{x^5}{5!} - \dfrac{x^7}{7!} + \ldots$	valid for all x
$\cos x = 1 - \dfrac{x^2}{2!} + \dfrac{x^4}{4!} - \dfrac{x^6}{6!} + \ldots$	valid for all x
$e^x = 1 + x + \dfrac{x^2}{2!} + \dfrac{x^3}{3!} + \ldots$	valid for all x
$\ln(1+x) = x - \dfrac{x^2}{2} + \dfrac{x^3}{3} - \dfrac{x^4}{4} + \ldots$	valid for $-1 < x \leq 1$
$(1+x)^n = 1 + nx + \dfrac{n(n-1)}{2!} x^2 + \ldots$	valid for $-1 < x < 1$
$\dfrac{1}{1+x} = 1 - x + x^2 - x^3 + \ldots$	valid for $-1 < x < 1$

The Taylor series for these basic functions can be used to deduce the Taylor series and the radius of convergence of related functions.

Example 3

Use the result

$$\frac{1}{1-x} = 1 + x + x^2 + x^3 + x^4 + \ldots, \text{ for } -1 < x < 1,$$

to write down the Taylor series for $\frac{1}{1-0.2x}$.

Solution

Substituting $0.2x$ for x in the above series gives

$$\frac{1}{1-0.2x} = 1 + 0.2x + 0.04 + 0.008 + \ldots$$

valid for $-1 < 0.2x < 1$.

The radius of convergence is therefore $-5 < x < 5$.

Exercise 2

1. (a) Write down the Taylor series for $\ln(1+x)$.

   (b) Hence deduce the Taylor series for $\ln(1 + 0.4x)$.

   (c) For what range of x is this series valid?

   (d) Use a graph plotter to graph $y = \ln(1 + 0.4x)$ and superimpose the graph of Taylor's fifth polynomial approximation to $\ln(1 + 0.4x)$. Does your answer to (c) seem reasonable?

2. (a) Write down the Taylor series for $\sin x$.

   (b) Hence deduce the Taylor series for $\sin(2x)$.

   (c) For what range of x is this series valid?

   (d) Use a graph plotter to graph $y = \sin(2x)$ and superimpose the graph of Taylor's ninth polynomial approximation to $\sin(2x)$. Does your answer to (c) seem reasonable?

3E. (a) Write $\frac{6}{2+x}$ in the form $a\left(\frac{1}{1+bx}\right)$.

   (b) Hence deduce the Taylor series for $\frac{6}{2+x}$.

   (c) What is the radius of convergence of this series?

3.5 Order of accuracy

In the previous section you found that while Taylor series were valid for all values of x for some functions, they were valid for only restricted values of x for other functions. Whatever the radius of convergence, it is impracticable to evaluate a series to infinity to determine the precise value of a function and so Taylor approximations are used instead. With an approximation there is an associated error and the usefulness of any approximation is to a certain extent determined by whether or not you can estimate this error without knowing the value of the function. To investigate the error, it is helpful to consider a function which **can** be evaluated easily.

The table gives **errors** for the rth approximation when using Taylor approximations for $\frac{1}{1-x}$.

	$x = 0.01$	$x = 0.02$	$x = 0.03$
$r = 1$	1.01×10^{-4}	4.08×10^{-4}	9.28×10^{-4}
$r = 2$	1.01×10^{-6}	8.16×10^{-6}	27.8×10^{-6}
$r = 3$	1.01×10^{-8}	16.3×10^{-8}	83.5×10^{-8}
$r = 4$	1.01×10^{-10}	32.7×10^{-10}	251×10^{-10}

(The values were obtained from a graphic calculator program and were rounded to 3 significant figures.)

> **(a)** What happens when you double the value of x in the first, second, third and fourth approximations?
>
> **(b)** What happens when you treble the value of x?
>
> **(c)** How does the degree of the approximation appear to be connected to the order of accuracy?
>
> **(d)** Produce a similar table for the function e^x for $r = 1$ and 2. Check the conjecture you made in (c).

You should have found that the order of accuracy of a Taylor approximation is one higher than the degree of the approximation (for small x). It is quite easy to see why this is the case for the function $\frac{1}{1-x}$ because the infinite series formed by continuing the pattern of the approximation (i.e. the Taylor series) is

$$\frac{1}{1-x} = 1 + x + x^2 + x^3 + x^4 + \dots$$

So the error when using Taylor's first approximation would be the sum to infinity of the series $x^2 + x^3 + x^4 + \dots$ (This can be thought of as the 'error series'.)

However, since x is small, the later terms in the error series become small very quickly, and so most of the error is likely to be contained in the first term.

It is easy to check that this is the case for the values in the table at the beginning of this section.

For example:

The error when using Taylor's first approximation for $\frac{1}{1-x}$ with $x = 0.02$ was 4.08×10^{-4}. (Check that this is indeed the difference between $\frac{1}{1-x}$ and $(1 + x)$ for $x = 0.02$.)

The first term in the error series for this approximation is x^2. For $x = 0.02$ this is 4×10^{-4}, which is very close to the error.

(a) How does the work above explain why Taylor's first approximation has second order accuracy?

(b) For Taylor's second approximation, what power of x will the first term of the error series contain? How does this explain the order of accuracy of Taylor's second approximation?

(c) Explain how similar reasoning will lead to the fact that the order of accuracy of a Taylor polynomial is always one more than the degree of the approximation, provided x is small.

The fact that Taylor's rth degree polynomial is an approximation with order of accuracy $r + 1$ means that the error is proportional to x^{r+1} and gives you some idea of what can be gained by evaluating higher degree approximations.

The error in Taylor's rth approximation to a function, centred on $x = 0$,

$$\text{error} = f(x) - \left(f(0) + f'(0)x + f''(0)\,\frac{x^2}{2!} + \ldots + f^{(r)}(0)\,\frac{x^r}{r!} \right),$$

is proportional to x^{r+1} for small values of x.

After working through this chapter you should:

1. know that for numerical differentiation:

$$f'(a) \approx \frac{f(a+h) - f(a)}{h}$$ is a first order approximation

$$f'(a) \approx \frac{f(a+h) - f(a-h)}{2h}$$ is a second order approximation

2. know how to evaluate Taylor's first and second approximations to a function centred on the point where $x = a$;

3. know how to evaluate Taylor's rth approximation, centred on the point where $x = 0$, for functions such as $\sin x$, $\cos x$, e^x, $\ln (1+x)$ and $(1+x)^n$;

4. understand the difference between a Taylor approximation and a Taylor series;

5. understand the term radius of convergence when applied to a Taylor series;

6. know that the error in a Taylor approximation of degree r, centred on $x = 0$, is proportional to x^{r+1} for small values of x.

Investigating radius of convergence

You should already have a program for investigating the radius of convergence of the Taylor series

$$\frac{1}{1-x} = 1 + x + x^2 + x^3 + \ldots$$

by evaluating the partial sum $S_r = 1 + x + x^2 + x^3 + \ldots + x^r$ for different values of r.

1.   Adjust the program to investigate the Taylor series

$$\frac{1}{1+x} = 1 - x + x^2 - x^3 + \ldots (-1)^r x^r + \ldots$$

What appears to be the radius of convergence of this series?

2.   Adjust the program to investigate the Taylor series

$$\ln(1+x) = x - \frac{x^2}{2} + \frac{x^3}{3} - \ldots (-1)^{r+1}\frac{x^r}{r} + \ldots$$

For what range of x does this series appear to be valid?

You can use a graph plotter to obtain a picture of how Taylor approximations become better approximations to the function (for values of x within the radius of convergence) as the value of r is increased.

3.   On the same axes graph $y = \frac{1}{1-x}$ and Taylor's second approximation $y = 1 + x + x^2$.

You get a visual picture of the range of x for which the approximation is reasonably good.

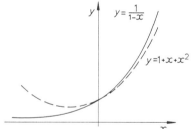

Now superimpose Taylor's third, fourth, fifth, ... approximations. (You will see how the approximation improves for values of x within the radius of convergence.)

4.   Use the graphical approach of question 3 to investigate the convergence of higher degree Taylor approximations to the function $\ln(1+x)$ and so confirm the radius of convergence you found in question 2.

5.   (a)   The series for $\sin x$ and e^x have similar properties as regards the radius of convergence. Investigate these series thoroughly, using the graphical approach of question 3.

        (b)   A Taylor series will only converge if at some point its terms start to get smaller. If $x = 5$, when will the terms of e^x start to get smaller? How does this help you explain the graphical results you obtained in part (a)?

1. (a) Work out Taylor's sixth approximation for $\cos x$, and hence write down Taylor's series for $\cos x$.

   (b) What is the radius of convergence of the series?

2. You have already worked out Taylor's fourth approximation for $\sqrt{(1 + x)}$:

   $$\sqrt{(1 + x)} \approx 1 + \frac{1}{2}x - \frac{1}{8}x^2 + \frac{1}{16}x^3 - \frac{5}{128}x^4$$

   (a) Write down Taylor's fourth approximation for $\sqrt{(1 - x)}$.

   (b) Use the polynomial for $\sqrt{(1 - x)}$ with the appropriate value of x to estimate $\sqrt{0.98}$ and so estimate $\sqrt{2}$ given that $7\sqrt{2} = \sqrt{98} = 10\sqrt{0.98}$. To how many significant figures is this estimate correct?

   (c) In a similar way use the polynomial for either $\sqrt{(1 + x)}$ or $\sqrt{(1 - x)}$ to estimate $\sqrt{3}$.

3. It is not possible to integrate $\sqrt{(1 + x^2)}$ algebraically.

   (a) Use the Taylor polynomial for $(1 + x)^n$ to work out Taylor's approximation up to the term in x^{10} for $\sqrt{(1 + x^2)}$.

   (b) Integrate this polynomial to obtain an estimate of $\int_0^{0.5} \sqrt{(1 + x^2)}\,dx$.

   (c) Investigate the accuracy of your answer by evaluating $\int_0^{0.5} \sqrt{(1 + x^2)}\,dx$. using Simpson's rule with different numbers of strips.

4. Historically, an important use of Taylor polynomials was to work out values for tables of logarithms and trigonometrical ratios.

   (a) Since you know the value of $\ln 1$, you can easily use one of the approximations for $\ln(1 + x)$ to estimate $\ln 1.1$. Do this for the second, third, … approximations until you are sure you have the value correct to 4 significant figures.

   (b) Repeat (a) for $\ln 1.2$, $\ln 1.4$ and $\ln 1.6$.

(continued)

5E   INVESTIGATION

You can only use the method of question 4 to evaluate ln x when $x < 2$ and the method will become lengthy when x gets near to 2.

Investigate how to obtain the natural logarithms of higher numbers.

Here are some ideas:

• You could calculate ln 2 by starting at, say, ln 1.6 and using the general Taylor approximation:

$$f(a + x) = f(a) + f'(a)x + f''(a)\,\frac{x^2}{2!} + f^{(3)}(a)\,\frac{x^3}{3!} + \ldots$$

(However, be careful, if you start with a value of ln 1.6 which you are sure is correct to 5 significant figures, your value for ln 2 will only be completely reliable to 4 significant figures.)

• You could use the the laws of logarithms, for example:

ln 10 = ln (2 x 2 x 2 x 1.25) = 3 ln 2 + ln 1.25

• You could write down a polynomial for ln $(1 - x)$.

Since $\ln\left(\frac{1+x}{1-x}\right) = \ln(1 + x) - \ln(1 - x)$, you can write down a polynomial for $\ln\left(\frac{1+x}{1-x}\right)$ and, by carefully choosing your values of x, you can evaluate some key logarithms.

Finally, remember that in the past this work would have had to be done by long multiplication, without the aid of a calculator!

4 Solving equations

4.1 Chaos

Population fluctuations in nature have been the subject of much study. Unexpected plagues of locusts can devastate farmland and lead to widespread famine, localised plagues of rats are still a cause for concern in many parts of the world and fish stocks can change from one year to the next in such a chaotic manner that it is difficult to persuade people to agree on what conservation measures to take.

Imagine a pond with fish. Let the fish population p be measured in such a way that $p = 0$ implies extinction and $p = 1$ implies total saturation. The population lies between these two extremes and varies according to an annual breeding cycle.

In the mid 1970s, an Australian scientist called Robert May proposed a simple mathematical population model for fish in such a pond. If this year's population is p_0, then next year's population will depend on two competing factors.

- Next year's population will depend on how many young this year's population produces. (The larger p_0 is, the more young are produced to boost next year's population.)

- If p_0 is large then food will be scarce, fish will starve and the population level will fall. On the other hand, if p_0 is small there will be plenty of food and the population will flourish.

Robert May proposed the following simple model for the yearly population figures.

$$p_1 = kp_0 (1 - p_0), \quad p_2 = kp_1 (1 - p_1), \quad p_3 = kp_2 (1 - p_2), \quad \dots$$

The number k, a constant called the 'boom' factor, can take any value from 0 to 4 and reflects the fish's ability to reproduce.

> **If the initial population $p_0 = 0.2$ and the boom factor $k = 3.2$, use May's population model to calculate the population figures for the next ten years.**

How the fish population behaves given a starting population, p_0, and a specific boom factor, k, is best illustrated on a graph.

The population may stabilise at a particular value.

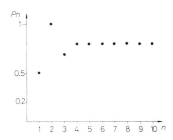

The population may oscillate between two (or more) values.

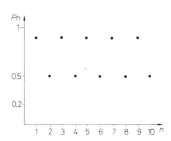

The population may fluctuate in an apparently random, or chaotic, way.

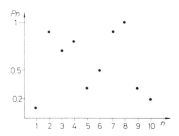

Write a short program for a computer or a graphic calculator to calculate and illustrate how population figures fluctuate according to May's model. (Help for this is given in the unit guide.)

(a) Investigate the iteration $p_{n+1} = kp_n(1-p_n)$, where $p_0 = 0.2$ and k takes the following values:

(i) $k = 0.5$ (ii) $k = 1$ (iii) $k = 2$ (iv) $k = 3$

(v) $k = 3.2$ (vi) $k = 3.5$ (vii) $k = 3.6$ (viii) $k = 4$

(b) Comment on what you find.

TASKSHEET 1E – *Step by step to chaos*

Although May's population model is far too simple to model real fish populations in real ponds, it does give a unique insight into the type of dynamic system which might apply.

The study of this type of problem has become an important branch of mathematics called **chaos** and has found many real applications. There are many popular books on the subject for those who are interested.

Similar iterations to the sequence generated by May's population model were looked at in the unit *Foundations* where they were used as a method for solving equations.

Discuss how to solve each of the following equations.

(a) $x + 1 = 4$

(b) $4x - 1 = 3x$

(c) $x^2 + 2 = 3x$

(d) $7 - x^5 = 3x$

(e) $\sin x + e^{x-5} = 0$

In attempting to solve the equations above you may have tried iteration for those you could not solve algebraically, or you may have suggested the use of a graph plotter to zoom in on the section of a graph where the solution lies. (Although this graphical method often provides a revealing insight into the problem, it is a relatively slow method of obtaining an accurate solution.)

As an alternative to either of the methods above, you may also have suggested a 'trial and improvement' method. Such a method is usually a mixture of two well-known numerical methods, **decimal search** and **bisection**.

The main purpose of this chapter is to compare and contrast the efficiency of numerical methods such as iteration, decimal search and bisection. Particular attention will be paid to what can go wrong.

4.2   Bisection and decimal search

The equation $\sin x + e^{x-5} = 0$ has an infinite number of solutions.

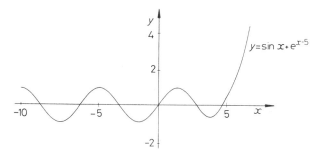

The graph of $y = \sin x$ is dominant for $x < 0$ and so there is an infinite number of roots close to $-n\pi$ where $n \in N$.

The graph of $y = e^{x-5}$ is dominant for $x > 2\pi$ and so there are no roots in this range of x.

The sketch shows there are two roots between $x = 0$ and $x = 2\pi$.

Investigating the value of the function $f(x) = \sin x + e^{x-5}$ shows that $f(4) < 0$ and $f(5) > 0$. It therefore follows that there must be a root between $x = 4$ and $x = 5$.

At this point you could sensibly adopt one of two strategies to narrow the interval within which the root must lie.

Decimal search:

Try $f(4.1)$, $f(4.2)$, etc ... until the functional value changes from negative to positive. In this example, $f(4.9) < 0$, but $f(5) > 0$ so the root must be between $x = 4.9$ and $x = 5.0$. You now evaluate $f(4.91)$, $f(4.92)$, etc... If you do this you will find that $f(4.96) < 0$ and $f(4.97) > 0$ and so the interval within which the root must lie has been narrowed to $4.96 \rightarrow 4.97$. The interval can be narrowed down to $4.967 \rightarrow 4.968$ after a further eight function calculations.

The equation $\sin x + e^{x-5} = 0$ is known to have a root between $x = 3$ and $x = 4$. **Suppose you use decimal search and find the root is in the interval $3.331 \rightarrow 3.332$.**

(a)   **How many function calculations would you have done?**

(b)   **If a root is known to lie between two consecutive integers, what are the maximum and the minimum number of function calculations needed to narrow the interval down to the third decimal place?**

(c)   **About how many function calculations would be needed 'on average' to narrow the interval down to the third decimal place using decimal search?**

Bisection

Evaluate the function at the mid-point of the interval. In this case, f(4.5) < 0 and so the interval within which the root must lie can be narrowed down to 4.5 → 5. You can now evaluate the function at the mid-point of the new interval and narrow the interval to 4.75 → 5 etc …

(a) If the interval from $x = a$ to $x = b$ is bisected n times, what is the length of the resulting sub-interval?

(b) You can use bisection to solve the equation $\sin x + e^{x-5} = 0$. Knowing that there is a root between $x = 3$ and $x = 4$, how many function calculations are necessary to reduce the interval length to 0.001?

(c) Which algorithm do you think is the more efficient; decimal search or bisection?

The efficiency of an algorithm for solving equations can be 'measured' by the number of function calculations which are necessary to obtain an estimate of the solution to a desired accuracy. The following tasksheet gives you further experience of the two methods.

 TASKSHEET 2 – *Bisection and decimal search*

If the root of an equation is known to lie between two consecutive integers then n applications of the method of bisection reduces the interval length to $\frac{1}{2^n}$.

Each 'application' of the method of decimal search reduces the interval by one decimal place. (An 'application' will require between 1 and 9 calculations of the equation.)

The method of bisection is on average more efficient than the method of decimal search.

A further application of the bisection method will always locate the root in an interval of half the size, and so will also halve the error. Although the decimal search method is not generally quite as efficient as the bisection method, it does have the advantage of always generating another decimal place for the solution.

4.3   Iteration

In *Foundations* you saw how an equation can be solved by iteration after first rearranging it into the form $x_0 = g(x)$. Repeated application of the iterative formula $x_{n+1} = g(x_n)$ will generate a sequence of numbers:

$$x_0, \ x_1, \ x_2, \ x_3, \ \ldots, \ x_n, \ x_{n+1}, \ \ldots$$

For example, the iterative formula, $x_{n+1} = \cos x_n$, can be used to solve the equation $x = \cos x$. A start value of $x = 1$ generates the sequence.

$$1, \ 0.540, \ 0.858, \ 0.654, \ 0.793, \ 0.701, \ 0.764, \ldots$$

> **Write a short program for a computer or a graphic calculator to generate and continue this sequence until you can state the solution to the equation correct to 3 decimal places.**

The solution to the equation $x = g(x)$ can be obtained graphically from the intersection of the graphs of $y = x$ and $y = g(x)$. These graphs can also be used with good effect to illustrate the behaviour of the iterative sequence generated by the formula $x_{n+1} = g(x_n)$.

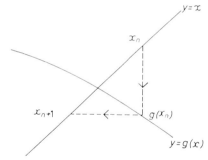

The iterative process goes through two stages in using one term to generate the next:

(i)   calculating $g(x_n)$ from x_n,

(ii)   letting $g(x_n)$ become x_{n+1}.

The two stages are shown as two arrowed lines in the diagram.

> (a)   **Sketch the graphs of $y = x$ and $y = \cos x$ on the same axes in the range $0.4 < x < 1.1$ and $0.4 < y < 1.1$.**
>
> (b)   **Show the two stages in the iteration which takes $x_0 = 1$ to $x_1 = 0.540$.**
>
> (c)   **On the same diagram, show the stages from:**
>
> $x_1 = 0.540$ to $x_2 = 0.858$
> $x_2 = 0.858$ to $x_3 = 0.654$
> $x_3 = 0.654$ to $x_4 = 0.793$
> etc ...

If the start value, x_0, is reasonably close to the root, then an iteration sequence can do one of four things. These are illustrated below on cobweb and staircase diagrams.

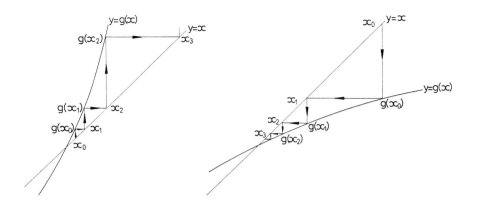

Staircase diagram with sequence diverging from the root.

Staircase diagram with sequence converging on the root.

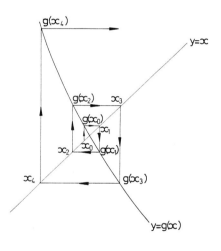

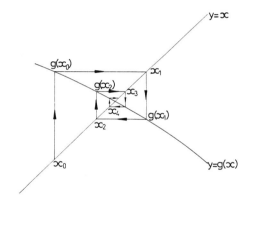

Cobweb diagram with sequence diverging from the root.

Cobweb diagram with sequence converging on the root.

   TASKSHEET 3 – *Investigating iteration*

48

If iteration is to be of any use as a method of solving equations you need to know

- why some sequences converge and why others do not

- how quickly an iteration sequence converges.

(Iteration is not a sensible method if the sequence converges very slowly on the root.)

If the root is $x = a$, then $a = g(a)$.

After n iterations the error is

$$|x_{n+1} - a|$$

The sequence will converge if the absolute value of the error is decreasing.

i.e. $\left| \dfrac{x_{n+1} - a}{x_n - a} \right| < 1$

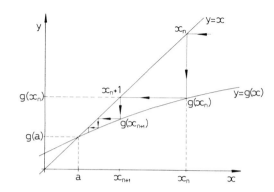

But $a = g(a)$ and $x_{n+1} = g(x_n)$

$$\Rightarrow \quad \frac{x_{n+1} - a}{x_n - a} = \frac{g(x_n) - g(a)}{x_n - a}$$

When $(x_n - a)$ is sufficiently small,

$$\frac{x_{n+1} - a}{x_n - a} \approx g'(a)$$

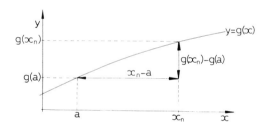

The sequence will therefore converge if the start value, x_0, is reasonably close to the root, a, and $|g'(a)| < 1$.

> **Under what conditions will iteration be a more efficient method of locating a root than bisection?**

An iterative sequence, $x_{n+1} = g(x_n)$, will converge to a root, $x = a$, only if
$$-1 < g'(a) < 1$$
Convergence will be fast when $g'(a)$ is close to zero and slow when $g'(a)$ is close to ± 1.

49

Exercise 1

1. (a) Solve $4x^2 - 12x + 9 = 0$ algebraically.

    (b) Try to find the root by iteration using the equation

    $$x = \frac{20x - 4x^2 - 9}{8}$$

    (c) For what range of starting values, x_0, does the sequence converge?

    (d) Explain why the iteration process is very slow.

2. (a) Investigate the iteration $x_{n+1} = \frac{1}{x_n}$.

    (b) What is the inverse function of $g(x) = \frac{1}{x}$?

    (c) How does your answer to (b) explain the behaviour of the iteration in (a)?

3. The fish population in a trout stream changes according to an annual breeding cycle. About 500 young fish are released into the stream each year to make up for the number caught by anglers. The farmer estimates that approximately 40% of the existing population are either caught or die of natural causes each year. The existing population is also boosted by natural breeding and the farmer estimates that this increases the population by 30% each year.

    (a) If x_n is the population at the start of the breeding season, write down an expression for x_{n+1}, the population 1 year later.

    (b) If $x_0 = 1000$, what would the population be after

        (i) 5 years   (ii) 10 years   (iii) 100 years

    (c) Repeat (b) with $x_0 = 8000$. Comment on your findings.

4.4   The Newton-Raphson method

Numerical methods for solving equations are not new. Isaac Newton (1642-1727) used a particular form of iteration to solve the problem of time in a planetary orbit. The basis of this method was as follows.

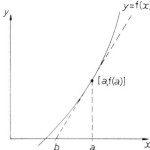

If you need to find the zero of a function, f(x), and you already know that a particular value, $x = a$, is close to the zero, then find the tangent to the graph of $y = f(x)$ at $(a, f(a))$. The value of x where the tangent crosses the x-axis (shown as b on the diagram) will be closer to the zero than a .

> **Explain why** $f'(a) = \dfrac{f(a)}{a - b}$ **and hence show that** $b = a - \dfrac{f(a)}{f'(a)}$.

Once an improved value has been obtained, you can use it as a new starting value and repeat the process.

Example 1

Solve the equation $x - \cos x = 0$ using the Newton-Raphson process, given that $x = 0.5$ is close to the root. (Find the root to 3 decimal places.)

Solution

$f(a) = a - \cos a$ and $f'(a) = 1 + \sin a$.

If a is close to the root, then $b = a - \dfrac{(a - \cos a)}{(1 + \sin a)}$ will be closer.

If $a = 0.5$ then $b = 0.5 - \dfrac{(0.5 - \cos 0.5)}{(1 + \sin 0.5)} = 0.7552$ (4 d.p.).

If $a = 0.7552$ then $b = 0.7391$ (4 d.p.)

If $a = 0.7391$ then $b = 0.7391$ (4 d.p.)

As this is the same as previous the value (to 4 d.p.) the root is 0.739 (3 d.p.).

> (a)   Solve the equation $x - \cos x = 0$ using the Newton-Raphson process starting at $x = 1$.
>
> (b)   Compare this method with an $x_{n+1} = \cos x_n$ iteration.

This method (using tangents) for solving an equation is named after the mathematician Joseph Raphson (1648-1715), who was a contemporary and close colleague of Isaac Newton. Although Newton was the first to invent the method, it was Raphson who refined it into a form recognisable as the method used today. Both mathematicians only used the method to solve polynomial equations. Thomas Simpson appears to have been the first to apply it to other functions when he extended the method in 1740.

Use a software package such as *The Newton-Raphson method* in *Numerical solutions to equations* to solve the equation $x - \cos x = 0$ starting at

(a) $x = 1$ (b) $x = 3$ (c) $x = 4.5$

The Newton-Raphson method gives a sequence of numbers x_1, x_2, x_3, ... which usually converges to a zero of a function f(x). The iterative formula which connects the terms of the sequence is

$$x_{n+1} = x_n - \frac{f(x_n)}{f'(x_n)}$$

Given a starting value x_1,

$$x_2 = x_1 - \frac{f(x_1)}{f'(x_1)}$$

$$x_3 = x_2 - \frac{f(x_2)}{f'(x_2)}$$

...

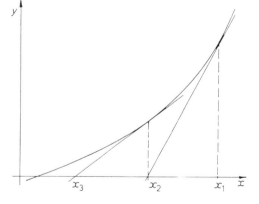

Providing the first estimate (x_1) is 'good' the method will usually converge very quickly to a zero of the function. A good first estimate is one such that the graph between the zero and the estimate is locally straight at all points and has no turning points. If the initial estimate is itself near a turning point, the Newton-Raphson method becomes unpredictable and will usually take you further from the zero.

The method is extremely efficient – you will often find that if x_1 is accurate to 1 decimal place, then x_2 is accurate to 2 decimal places, x_3 to 4 decimal places, x_4 to 8 and x_5 to 16 decimal places!

One major disadvantage of the method is the need for differentiation. (It is easy to make a mistake when differentiating a complicated function.)

You saw in Chapter 3 that $\dfrac{f(x+h)-f(x)}{h}$ is a first order approximation to

$f'(x)$ and that $\dfrac{f(x+h)-f(x-h)}{2h}$ is a second order approximation.

Explain why the iterative formula $x_{n+1} = x_n - \dfrac{h\,f(x_n)}{f(x_n+h)-f(x_n)}$,

where h is small, can be used in place of $x_{n+1} = x_n - \dfrac{f(x_n)}{f'(x_n)}$

TASKSHEET 4 – *The Newton-Raphson method*

A numerical approximation can be used in the Newton-Raphson method in place of the derivative. The iteration formula then becomes:

$$x_{n+1} = x_n - \dfrac{h\,f(x_n)}{f(x_n+h)-f(x_n)}$$ with first order numerical gradient.

The method is very efficient unless $f'(x)$ is zero (or close to zero) at the root.

Exercise 2

1. (a)   Use the Newton-Raphson method to find the three zeros of the function

$$f(x) = x^3 - 8x^2 + 16x - 4$$

   (b)   Which zero do you reach if you have a starting value of

   (i)   3.70   (ii)   3.75   (iii)   3.77   (iv)   3.80?

   (c)   Try other starting values in the range 3.70 to 3.80. Why is it not a good idea to use starting values in this range?

After working through this chapter you should:

1.   know how to solve equations by

   - the method of bisection;
   - the decimal search method;
   - $x = g(x)$ iteration;
   - the Newton-Raphson method;

2.   appreciate the respective advantages of the different methods;

3.   understand some of the factors affecting speed of convergence to a root;

4.   appreciate the conditions under which a method may fail to give convergence to a root;

5.   have some understanding of the term 'chaos' in its mathematical context.

Step by step to chaos

The iteration formula $p_{n+1} = 3.2 \, p_n \, (1 - p_n)$ settles down to oscillate between two values, $p = 0.513 \ldots$ and $p = 0.799 \ldots$

In a similar way, the formula $p_{n+1} = 3.5 \, p_n \, (1 - p_n)$ settles down to oscillate (or cycle) between four values; it goes from $p = 0.382 \ldots$ to $p = 0.826$ to $p = 0.500 \ldots$ to $p = 0.874 \ldots$ and back to $p = 0.382 \ldots$ repeating the cycle.

The first iteration is called a **two-cycle attractor** and the second is a **four-cycle attractor**. In 1976 Robert May suggested plotting attractor values against k for the iteration formula $p_{n+1} = kp_n \, (1 - p_n)$.

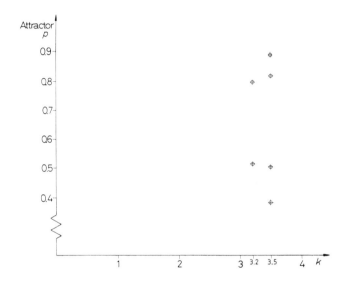

1. Extend the graph shown above by plotting the results for $k = 0.5, 1, 2, 3, 3.2,$ and 3.5. (You investigated the iterations for these values of k earlier in the text.)

2. Write a short program for a computer or a graphic calculator to obtain a full plot for $0 \le k \le 4$ where k is varied in steps of 0.1. (Help is given in the unit guide.)

In the mid 1970s Robert May asked his graduate students to explain what happens when k gets bigger than 3.57. You should have found that for values of k greater than 3.57 you get a plot of randomly distributed points which lie within certain numerical limits. The behaviour is **not** cyclic as no repetition takes place. This limiting behaviour of the iteration is said to be **chaotic** and the diagram you obtain is called a **bifurcation diagram.**

3. Adapt your program to produce a bifurcation diagram for the iteration formula

$$p_{n+1} = k(p_n^3 - 3p_n^2 + 2p_n)$$

(continued)

55

In 1976, Mitchell Feigenbaum, a leading theorist of chaos, investigated bifurcation diagrams while working at Los Alamos. He looked at the length of step in k between the start of one attractor type and the start of the next attractor type. (This step length is shown as h in the diagram.)

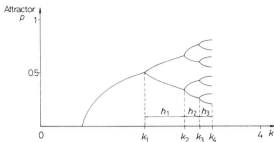

4.   By using the bifurcation diagrams from questions 2 and 3, estimate the step lengths, h_1, h_2 and h_3 for each diagram. (Modify the program to 'Zoom' in on part of the diagram from $x = 3.4$ to $x = 3.6$. If you are using a graphic calculator then do not try to obtain answers to more than 2 decimal places.)

5.   Use your estimates from question 4 to estimate the ratios

$$\frac{h_1}{h_2} \text{ and } \frac{h_2}{h_3} \text{ for each diagram.}$$

Feigenbaum found that the ratio $\dfrac{h_{n-1}}{h_n}$ tended to 4.6692016090 (10 d.p.)

It approached this limit quite quickly and this ratio is now referred to as δ, the Feigenbaum constant.

Feigenbaum's discovery can be proved for any iteration

$$p_{n+1} = f(p)_n \quad f(p_n)$$

based on a 'hump-backed' function, $f(p)$, in the interval $0 \le p \le 1$.

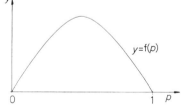

The importance of the discovery of Feigenbaum's constant lay in the fact that it enables the value of k beyond which chaos starts to be calculated with precision. The importance of the discovery can be seen in its effect upon sciences and areas of study as diverse as the study of heart attacks, a new theory about Jupiter's red spot, the economics of the stock market, fluid engineering, fish stocks in the North Sea, and many more.

6.   (a)   If $k_1 = 1$ and $h_1 = 2$, estimate k_2, k_3 and k_4.

       (b)   Show that $k_n \approx 1 + 2 + \dfrac{2}{\delta} + \dfrac{2}{\delta^2} + \dots + \dfrac{2}{\delta^{n-2}}$

       (c)   Show that the sum of this series to infinity is 3.5451 (4 d.p.).

       (d)   What is the significance of this value?

Bisection and decimal search

For this tasksheet you will need to write your own computer program and/or use the software package *Numerical solutions of equations*.

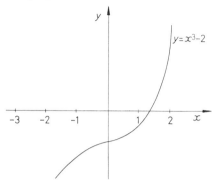

1.   Use the bisection method to solve the equation $x^3 - 2 = 0$. Record how many steps it takes to find the root, given that the graph of $y = x^3 - 2$ passes through the points $(1, -1)$ and $(2, 6)$, if you require an accuracy of

(a)   3 decimal places

(b)   6 decimal places.

2.   Repeat question 1 using decimal search and comment on the relative efficiency of the two methods.

3.   Investigate the relative efficiency of the two methods (bisection and decimal search) in solving $x^2 - x - 3 = 0$ correct to

(a)   3 decimal places

(b)   6 decimal places.

4.   Repeat question 3 for the equation $e^x - \sin x - 4 = 0$.

Investigating iteration

An equation such as $x = \cos x$ can be solved only by numerical methods. It is, in fact, sensible to investigate the efficiency of iteration by considering an equation such as a simple quadratic which can be solved algebraically. For this tasksheet you will need to write your own computer program and/or use the software package *Numerical solutions of equations*.

1.   The quadratic equation $x^2 - 2x - 5 = 0$ can be rearranged into the form $x = \dfrac{5}{x-2}$

    (a)   Solve the equation

$$x^2 - 2x - 5 = 0$$

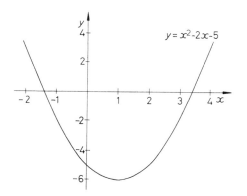

         by completing the square (or otherwise) and verify that the equation has two solutions,

$$1 \pm \sqrt{6}$$

    (b)   Use a software package with graphics to investigate the sequence generated by the iteration $x_{n+1} = \dfrac{5}{x_n - 2}$.

    (c)   Use a numerical method (or otherwise) to evaluate the derivatives,

         $g'(1 + \sqrt{6})$ and $g'(1 - \sqrt{6})$ where $g(x) = \dfrac{5}{x-2}$.

2.   The quadratic equation, $x^2 - 2x - 5 = 0$, can be rearranged to give,

    $x = \surd\,(2x + 5),\quad x = -\surd\,(2x + 5),\quad x = \dfrac{x^2 - 5}{2}\ ,\ \dots$

    (a)   Think of at least one other rearrangement.

    (b)   Investigate the sequences generated by each of the above arrangements as well as your own.

    (c)   Use a numerical method (or otherwise) to evaluate the derivatives,
         $g'(1 + \sqrt{6})$ and $g'(1 - \sqrt{6})$ where

         $g(x) = \surd\,(2x + 5),\quad g(x) = -\surd\,(2x + 5),\quad$ etc ...

3.   Can you see any connection between the behaviour of an $x = g(x)$ iteration and the value of $g'(x)$ at the root?

The Newton-Raphson method

There is an obvious advantage to using a numerical approximation for the derivative in the Newton-Raphson method. You do not have to differentiate the function! There are, however, certain questions you should ask.

- Is the advantage at the expense of accuracy and/or efficiency?

- Is it much more efficient to use a second order approximation to the derivative rather than a first order approximation?

1. (a) Write a short program on a computer or a graphic calculator (help is given in the unit guide) to solve the equation $x - \cos x = 0$ to 4 decimal places by the Newton-Raphson method, starting at $x = 1$, with

   (i) the derived function;

   (ii) a first order numerical method for the derivative;

   (iii) a second order numerical method for the derivative.

   Compare the efficiency of the three methods.

   (b) Repeat part (a) with different starting points and different functions.

   (c) How would you answer the questions posed at the top of this page?

You have seen that the $x = g(x)$ iteration will converge to a root, a, only when $|g'(a)| < 1$. At each stage of the iteration the error is then $(x_{n+1} - a) \approx g'(a)(x_n - a)$. The $x = g(x)$ iteration method is therefore very efficient when $|g'(a)|$ is close to zero.

The Newton-Raphson formula, $x_{n+1} = x_n - \dfrac{f(x_n)}{f'(x_n)}$, is of the form $x_{n+1} = g(x_n)$, where $g(x) = x - \dfrac{f(x)}{f'(x)}$

2E. (a) If $g(x) = x - \dfrac{f(x)}{f'(x)}$, then $g'(x) = \dfrac{f(x)\, f''(x)}{f'(x)^2}$.

   This statement can be proved using the quotient rule for differentiation. If you are familiar with this rule show that the statement is correct.

   (b) The iteration will be very efficient if $g'(a) \approx 0$.

   (i) Why would you expect $g'(a) \approx 0$ whatever form the function $f(x)$ takes?

   (ii) What feature(s) of the graph of $y = f(x)$ might make the Newton-Raphson method less efficient?

1. A teacher says to her class, 'Look up any word in the dictionary and I guarantee that I can tell you which word it is by asking no more than twenty questions'.

   How can she be so sure? What type of questions does she ask?

2. (a) Investigate the iteration $x_{n+1} = \dfrac{(2x_n + 1)}{(x_n - 2)}$

   (b) Find $g^{-1}(x)$ if $g(x) = \dfrac{(2x + 1)}{(x - 2)}$

   (c) How does your answer to (b) explain the behaviour of the iteration in (a)?

3. (a) Try solving the equation $x^3 = 2x^2 + 4x - 8$ using the Netwon-Raphson method.

   (b) The equation has two roots, $x = 2$ and $x = -2$. Explain why the method is much more efficient at locating the $x = -2$ root than the $x = 2$ root.

4. Consider Robert May's population model, $p_{n+1} = kp_n(1 - p_n)$ as an $x_{n+1} = kx_n(1 - x_n)$ iteration.

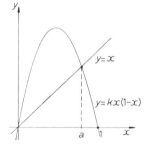

   (a) Use a graph plotter to help you sketch graphs of $y = x$ and $y = kx(1 - x)$ for values of k in the range $0 < k < 4$.

   (b) Use 'staircase' diagrams to explain why the iteration starts by converging on the root $x = 0$ for small values of k, switches to $x = a$ as k increases, and then starts behaving in a less predictable way as k gets closer to 4.

   (c) For what specific value of k does the iteration stop converging on $x = 0$ and start converging on the root $x = a$. (Hint: consider $g'(0)$ where $g(x) = kx(1 - x)$.)

   (d) (i) Find the value a for which $g(a) = a$ **and** $g'(a) = -1$.

       (ii) For what value of k does this occur?

       (iii) Explain why the iteration no longer converges on a root when k is increased beyond this value.

5   *Differential equations*

5.1   Euler's method

Prior to the nineteenth century, various methods were developed for solving differential equations **analytically**. With the advent of increasingly powerful computers, a good deal of current research is concerned with finding **numerical** solutions.

This is a particularly important area of research as most differential equations cannot be solved analytically. Many of the differential equations arising from astronomy, for example, can be solved only by numerical methods. A famous example was the work of Adams and Le Verrier on the orbit of Uranus which led to the discovery of the planet Neptune. Using numerical methods to solve the differential equations arising from the problem, they successfully predicted a numerically defined direction in space where a telescope should be aimed at a specific time to view the new planet. Much early numerical work was, in fact, performed by astronomers, but nowadays numerical methods are applied to problems in physics, chemistry, biology, engineering, economics, weather forecasting, analysis of population growth, etc...

You will already have done some work on differential equations in the unit *Mathematical methods* and you should be familiar with the step-by-step method of solution. This numerical method for solving differential equations is also referred to as **Euler's method**, named after the Swiss mathematician Leonhard Euler (1707-1783).

Euler's method is based on Taylor's first approximation to a function.

If $\frac{dy}{dx} = g(x)$ and $y = y_0$ when $x = x_0$,
then $y_1 = y_0 + hg(x_0)$
when $x_1 = x_0 + h$

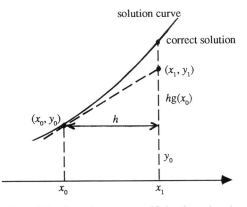

This will be a good approximation to the value of the function at $x=x_1$ if the function is locally straight over the interval x_0 to x_1. This process can be applied repeatedly to approximate the value of the function at $x_2, x_3 \dots$

$$y_2 = y_1 + hg(x_1) \text{ and } x_2 = x_1 + h$$
$$y_3 = y_2 + hg(x_2) \text{ and } x_3 = x_2 + h$$
$$\vdots$$
$$y_{n+1} = y_n + hg(x_n) \text{ and } x_{n+1} = x_n + h$$

The accuracy of a numerical method such as this can be investigated by applying it to an equation which can be solved analytically.

For example, the differential equation
$$\frac{dy}{dx} = 3x^2$$
starting at $x = 1$, $y = 1$ has solution $y = x^3$ and so $y = 8$ when $x = 2$.

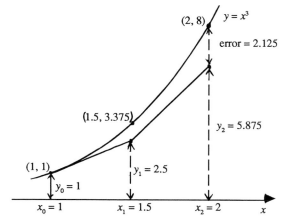

Euler's method with $h = \frac{1}{2}$ gives

n	x_n	y_n
0	1	1
1	1.5	2.5
2	2	5.875

The precise value of y is 8 when x is 2, so the error in using the numerical method is $8 - 5.875 = 2.125$.

The accuracy can be improved by using a much smaller step length. You could, for example, have 1000 steps of length 0.001 instead of just 2 steps of length $\frac{1}{2}$. This would be impossibly tedious to calculate by hand. The very repetitiveness of the process, however, means that you can write a short program to enable a computer to carry out the calculations very quickly. (See the program *Euler's method* in the unit guide.)

Complete the following table, recording the error to 4 s.f.

Step	Estimated value of y when $x = 2$	Error
1/2	5.875	2.125
1/4		
1/8		
1/16		
1/20		

(a)   What happens to the error (approximately) as the step length is halved?

(b)   By considering the steps $\frac{1}{2}$ and $\frac{1}{20}$, decide what happens when the step length is divided by 10.

(c)   What appears to be the order of approximation of Euler's method?

(d)   Make an educated guess as to how many steps might be needed to reduce the error to 0.0001. (Do not check this on a graphic calculator!)

5.2 Improving accuracy

There are two visually obvious ways of improving accuracy.

Mid-point Euler:

Instead of using the gradient at the initial point of the step, use the gradient at the mid-point.

If $\frac{dy}{dx} = g(x)$ and $y = y_0$ when $x = x_0$,

then $y_1 = y_0 + hg(x_0 + \frac{h}{2})$

and $x_1 = x_0 + h$

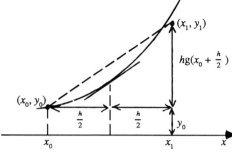

Improved Euler:

Instead of using the gradient at the initial point only, use the average of the gradients at the initial point and the end point of the step.

If $\frac{dy}{dx} = g(x)$ and $y = y_0$ when $x = x_0$,

then $y_1 = y_0 + h \dfrac{g(x_0) + g(x_0 + h)}{2}$

and $x_1 = x_0 + h$

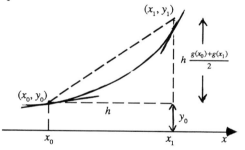

Only a small adjustment is needed to alter a computer program for solving differential equations by Euler's method to one for solving differential equations by either of these improved methods. (See the programs *Mid-point Euler* and *Improved Euler* in the unit guide)

> For each of the two improved methods, complete a table of errors similar to the one completed for Euler's method in the previous section (use the same differential equation).
>
> What appears to be the order of approximation of:
>
> (a)   the mid-point Euler method;
>
> (b)   the improved Euler method?
>
> Which method do you prefer and why?

   TASKSHEET 1 – *Investigating error*

Numerical methods for solving differential equations start at a known point (x_0, y_0) and use a recurrence relation to estimate the subsequent points of the solution curve: $(x_1, y_1), (x_2, y_2), \ldots$

For $\frac{dy}{dx} = g(x)$ and small h, the recurrence relations are as follows.

Euler's method: $\quad y_{n+1} = y_n + hg(x_n) : x_{n+1} = x_n + h$

Mid-point Euler: $\quad y_{n+1} = y_n + hg(x_n + \frac{h}{2}) : x_{n+1} = x_n + h$

Improved Euler: $\quad y_{n+1} = y_n + h \, \dfrac{g(x_n) + g(x_n + h)}{2} : \quad x_{n+1} = x_n + h$

Euler's method is a first order approximation.

The mid-point Euler and improved Euler methods are both second order approximations.

Example 1

If $\frac{dy}{dx} = \sin(x^2)$ and $(x_0, y_0) = (0, 0)$, find y when $x = 1.5$ using the mid-point Euler method with:

(a)   3 steps of length 0.5;   (b)   6 steps of length 0.25.

Solution

(a) $y_{n+1} = y_n + 0.5 \, g(x_n + 0.25)$
       $x_{n+1} = x_n + 0.5$
       with $g(x) = \sin(x^2)$ and $(x_0, y_0) = (0, 0)$

n	x_n	y_n
0	0	0
1	0.5	0.03123
2	1.0	0.29788
3	1.5	0.79786

(b) $y_{n+1} = y_n + 0.25 \, g(x_n + 0.125)$
       $x_{n+1} = x_n + 0.25$
       with $g(x) = \sin(x^2)$ and $(x_0, y_0) = (0, 0)$

n	x_n	y_n
0	0	0
1	0.25	0.00391
2	0.50	0.03895
3	0.75	0.13414
4	1.00	0.30739
5	1.25	0.54583
6	1.50	0.78316

Example 2

Use your answers to (a) and (b) in Example 1, together with the knowledge that the mid-point Euler is a second order approximation, to obtain an improved estimate of y when $x = 1.5$.

Solution

A second order approximation has the property that if you halve the step length (and double the number of steps) then the error is reduced to approximately a quarter of what it was.

So the value of y when $x = 1.5$ is given by

$$(y - 0.79786) : (y - 0.78316) = 4 : 1$$

$$\Rightarrow y - 0.79786 = 4(y - 0.78316)$$
$$\Rightarrow y = 0.77826$$

Thus if $\frac{dy}{dx} = \sin(x^2)$ and $(x_0, y_0) = (0, 0)$, then $y = 0.77826$ when $x = 1.5$.

Note that this problem could not have been solved by analysis so it is not possible to quantify the error precisely.

> **You may wonder if it is appropriate to quote a five significant figure value for y. How accurate do you think this answer is?**
>
> **If you run a computer program with 1500 steps of 0.001 to solve this problem, then you will probably feel confident that your result is accurate. Do this and see how accurate an answer $y = 0.77826$ really is.**

Exercise 1

1. In Example 1, $\frac{dy}{dx} = \sin x^2$ and $(x_0, y_0) = (0, 0)$.

   Given that the improved Euler method gives $(x, y) = (1.5, 0.73896)$ with step length $h = 0.5$ and $(x, y) = (1.5, 0.76841)$ with step length $h = 0.25$, use the fact that the improved Euler is a second order approximation to calculate a more accurate value for y when $x = 1.5$.

2. A calculator with a facility for solving differential equations by a numerical method gave $(1, 1.375)$ as a solution to a differential equation with step length $h = 0.2$, and gave $(1, 1.417)$ when the step length was $h = 0.1$.

   Given that the analytic solution is $(1, 1.460)$, say if you think the calculator uses Euler's method or the mid-point Euler method. Justify your answer.

5.3   Fourth order Runge-Kutta

When comparing the mid-point Euler method for solving differential equations with the improved Euler method, you will have noticed that the methods produce different solutions with the correct solution being somewhere between the two. You will, moreover, have noticed that while both methods have order of accuracy 2, the mid-point method produces a smaller error than the improved Euler method for a given step length. In fact, the error of the mid-point Euler method is approximately half that of the improved Euler method.

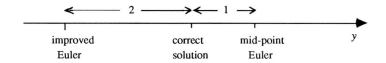

You can use this knowledge to improve your estimate of the solution to a differential equation.

Example 3

Using a step length of $h = 0.5$, the mid-point Euler method gives $(1.5, 0.79786)$ as a solution to the differential equation:

$$\frac{dy}{dx} = \sin x^2 \text{ with } (x_0, y_0) = (0, 0)$$

and the improved Euler method gives a solution of $(1.5, 0.73896)$. Use these results to calculate an improved estimate.

Solution

The error of the mid-point Euler method is approximately half that of the improved Euler method.

So the value of y when $x = 1.5$ is given by

$$(y - 0.73896) : (0.79786 - y) = 2 : 1.$$

0.73896		y	0.79786
(improved)			(mid-point)

$$\Rightarrow y - 0.73896 = 2 (0.79786 - y)$$

$$\Rightarrow y = \frac{2 \times 0.79786 + 0.73896}{3}$$

$$\Rightarrow y = 0.77823$$

Thus if $\frac{dy}{dx} = \sin (x^2)$ and $(x_0, y_0) = (0, 0)$, then $y = 0.77823$ when $x = 1.5$.

66

You will have seen that an accurate solution to this problem is $y = 0.77824$ (to 5 d.p.). Taking a weighted average of the mid-point Euler and the improved Euler methods is therefore a remarkably good numerical method for solving differential equations.

 TASKSHEET 2 – *The weighted average*

The weighted average of the mid-point Euler and the improved Euler methods is called the **fourth order Runge-Kutta** method.

If $\frac{dy}{dx} = g(x)$ and $y = y_0$ when $x = x_0$, then

$$y_1 = y_0 + h \times \frac{g(x_0) + 4g(x_{0.5}) + g(x_1)}{6}$$

where

$$x_{0.5} = x_0 + \frac{h}{2}$$

and

$$x_1 = x_0 + h$$

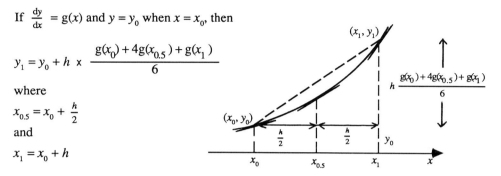

This method for calculating the approximate solution to a differential equation is a fourth order approximation (i.e. you reduce the error by a factor of sixteen (2^4) by halving the step length).

> **If $\frac{dy}{dx} = g(x)$, the recurrence relation for the fourth order Runge-Kutta method is:**
>
> $$y_{n+1} = y_n + h \frac{g(x_n) + 4g(x_n + \frac{h}{2}) + g(x_n + h)}{6}$$
>
> $$x_{n+1} = x_n + h$$

When a differential equation represents a rate of change with respect to time you may need to estimate what a quantity was in the past rather than what it will be in the future.

For example, suppose the speed of an object at time t is given by $\frac{ds}{dt} = e^{-t^2}$ and that $s = 3$ when $t = 0$.

> **Use the fourth order Runge-Kutta method with a negative step to estimate s to 4 decimal places when $t = -2$.**

67

Exercise 2

1. For the differential equation $\frac{dy}{dx} = e^{-x^2}$, three students are asked to find the value of y when $x = 1$, given that the solution curve passes through $(0, 0)$. The first student uses the mid-point Euler method with a step length of 0.25. The second uses the improved Euler method, also with a step length of 0.25. Their results are shown below.

	Step	y when $x = 1$
Mid-point Euler	0.25	0.74874713
Improved Euler	0.25	0.74298410

   The third student uses these results to calculate the fourth order Runge-Kutta estimate. Show how she does this.

2. A solution curve for $\frac{dy}{dx} = \sin x$ passes through the point $(0, 0)$. The fourth order Runge-Kutta method with a step length of 1 gives $y = 1.416653583$ when $x = 2$. When the step length is reduced to $\frac{1}{3}$, the solution is $y = 1.416152927$.

   (a) If you can assume that the actual value is smaller than both these values of y, then you can use the fact that the method is a fourth order approximation to calculate the actual value of y. Show how you can do this by calculating, from the approximations given, the value of y when $x = 2$.

   (b) Solve the differential equation algebraically and explain why the method suggested in (a) does not result in a precise solution.

3. A solution curve for the differential equation $\frac{dy}{dx} = \sin(x^2)$ passes through the point $(0, 0)$. The fourth order Runge-Kutta method is used to find y when $x = 1.5$. The following results are obtained.

Step	Value of y
0.1	0.778237903
0.01	0.778237804

   Explain why it might be reasonable to conclude that the second result is accurate to the 9 decimal places shown.

5.4　Extending the method

You may have noticed a similarity between the methods used for calculating numerical solutions to differential equations and those used for numerical integration. This is not surprising given that differential equations are solved analytically by integration! The equivalence between the methods is illustrated below:

Euler's method ⟷ **First ordinate rule**	*First order approximations*
Improved Euler ⟷ **Trapezium rule**	⎫
Mid-point Euler ⟷ **Mid-ordinate rule**	⎬ *Second order approximations* ⎭
Runge-Kutta ⟷ **Simpson's rule**	*Fourth order approximations*

The Euler method is, of course, based on Taylor's first (linear) approximation. You may have thought that the obvious extension to this is to use Taylor's second (quadratic) approximation (or his third, fourth, etc ...).

Consider Taylor's second approximation:

$$f(a + h) \approx f(a) + h\, f'(a) + \frac{h^2}{2!}\, f''(a)$$

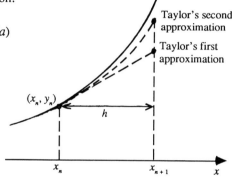

Substituting x_n for a and y_n for $f(a)$, and $g(x)$ for $f'(x)$ and $g'(x)$ for $f''(x)$, gives the recurrence relation:

$$y_{n+1} = y_n + hg(x_n) + \frac{h^2}{2!} g'(x_n)$$

$$x_{n+1} = x_n + h$$

Similarly, Taylor's third approximation would produce the recurrence relation:

$$y_{n+1} = y_n + hg(x_n) + \frac{h^2}{2!} g'(x_n) + \frac{h^3}{3!} g''(x_n) : x_{n+1} = x_n + h$$

with higher degree approximations following the same pattern.

The disadvantage of this method is that you have to differentiate the gradient function, $g(x)$, at least once.

If, for example, $g(x) = \sin(x^2)$

then $g'(x) = 2x \cos(x^2)$
$g''(x) = 2 \cos(x^2) - 4x^2 \sin(x^2)$
etc ...

(The first differentiation is an example of the chain rule and the second differentiation requires the use of the product rule.)

Because repeated differentiation can be tedious, Taylor polynomials are not often used to solve differential equations.

> **Write down a recurrence relation for solving $\frac{dy}{dx} = \cos x$ based on:**
>
> **(a)** **Taylor's second approximation;**
>
> **(b)** **Taylor's third approximation.**

This chapter has looked at the accuracy of some of the various numerical methods for solving differential equations. It should be pointed out that these methods are based on first order differential equations of the type $\frac{dy}{dx} = g(x)$.

Many differential equations are, however, functions of both x and y. For example, $\frac{dy}{dx} = -xy$.

While this presents no problem for Euler's method, the other three methods have to use an interim estimate of y to produce a more accurate estimate. Although this reduces the absolute accuracy of the approximation, the order of accuracy remains more or less the same.

 TASKSHEET 3E – *Extending the method*

5.5   Avoiding disaster

A numerical method can go wrong if you choose a step length which is too small for your calculator or computer to cope with. For this reason, methods such as the fourth order Runge-Kutta are very useful because a very small step length is not needed and so the type of rounding errors discussed in Chapter 1 are avoided.

Sometimes, the solution to a differential equation has features which affect both analytic and numerical methods.

> **What happens if you try to use the improved Euler method with** $(x_0, y_0) = (-1, 1)$ **to solve the differential equation** $\frac{dy}{dx} = -\frac{1}{x^2}$ **for** $x = 2$ **using:**
>
> (a)   **step length** $h = 0.3$;
>
> (b)   **step length** $h = 0.2$?
>
> **Explain why the method fails.**

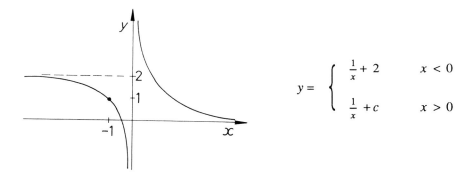

$$y = \begin{cases} \dfrac{1}{x} + 2 & x < 0 \\[2mm] \dfrac{1}{x} + c & x > 0 \end{cases}$$

You may find that a numerical method fails, not necessarily because you choose a step length which is too large or too small, but because you have failed to notice an important feature of the graph such as an asymptote. However, such problems are the exception rather than the rule and numerical methods yield excellent results provided reasonable care is taken.

After working through this chapter you should:

1. know how to use a numerical method to solve differential equations of the type $\frac{dy}{dx} = g(x)$;

2. know that for small step lengths:

    *   Euler's method is a first order approximation;
    *   the improved Euler method is a second order approximation;
    *   the mid-point Euler method is a second order approximation;
    *   the fourth order Runge-Kutta method is a fourth order approximation;

3. know that the fourth order Runge-Kutta method is a weighted average of the improved Euler and the mid-point Euler methods;

4. appreciate the connection between the numerical methods for solving differential equations and those for integration.

Investigating error

The Euler method appears to be a first order approximation.

1.   Explain what this statement means.

The improved Euler and the mid-point Euler methods both appear to be approximations with order of accuracy 2 (i.e. second order approximations).

2.   Explain what this statement means.

Both statements are conjectures based on just one example: the differential equation

$$\frac{dy}{dx} = 3x^2 \text{ starting at } x = 1 \text{ and } y = 1.$$

You really need to test these conjectures on other functions before being prepared to accept them as true without a proof. (You will need an appropriate computer program for questions 3 and 4.)

3.   The differential equation $\frac{dy}{dx} = -2x^3 + x + 1$ starting at $x = 0$, $y = 10$ has solution

$y = -\frac{1}{2}x^4 + \frac{1}{2}x^2 + x + 10$. So $y = 6$ when $x = 2$.

If you use the mid-point Euler method with 8 steps of $\frac{1}{4}$, you obtain the estimated value $y = 6.0625$, so the error is 0.0625. This result, together with other errors using different steps and methods, is shown below.

Errors

Step	Euler's method	Improved Euler	Mid-point Euler
1/2	3	0.5	0.25
1/4	1.625	0.125	**0.0625**
1/20	0.345	0.005	0.0025
1/40	0.174	0.00125	0.000625

Use a computer program to confirm at least one other result in the table and comment on what the order of accuracy appears to be for each method of approximation.

4.   Both the cases investigated have been polynomials. It might be true that what you noticed only applies to polynomials! Complete similar tables of errors for:

(a) $\frac{dy}{dx} = \cos x$ starting at $(0, 9.85888)$ if you require y when $x = 3$
       ($y = \sin x + 9.85888$);

(b) $\frac{dy}{dx} = 2e^{2x-3}$ starting at $(1.5, 6.40185)$ if you require y when $x = 3.5$
       ($y = e^{2x-3} + 5.40185$);

(c)   any differential equation you choose. (Remember that it must be one you can solve by analysis so that you can calculate the error.)

The weighted average

1.   Show that the weighted average of the mid-point Euler:

$$y_{n+1} = y_n + hg\left(x_n + \frac{h}{2}\right)$$

and the improved Euler,

$$y_{n+1} = y_n + h\,\frac{g(x_n) + g(x_n + h)}{2}$$

weighted 2:1 in favour of the mid-point Euler method, will be defined by the recurrence relation:

$$y_{n+1} = y_n + h\,\frac{g(x_n) + 4g(x_n + \frac{h}{2}) + g(x_n + h)}{6}$$

2.   Write a short program for a computer or graphic calculator to solve the differential equation $\frac{dy}{dx} = g(x)$ using the recurrence relation:

$$y_{n+1} = y_n + h\,\frac{g(x_n) + 4g(x_n + \frac{h}{2}) + g(x_n + h)}{6} \quad \text{and } x_{n+1} = x_n + h$$

and starting at (x_0, y_0).

3.   Use the program for question 2 to solve the differential equation

$$\frac{dy}{dx} = 3x^2\text{, starting at } (1, 1).$$

This has solution $y = x^3$, and so $y = 8$ when $x = 2$. Complete the following table of errors in estimating y when $x = 2$.

Step	Error
1	
1/2	
1/4	
1/8	

4.   Investigate the error when the method of question 2 is used to solve $\frac{dy}{dx} = g(x)$ when $g(x)$ is:

(a)   any quadratic function;   (b)   any cubic function;

(c)   any quartic function;   (d) $\cos x$ and when $(x_0, y_0) = (0, 0)$ and $x = 2$.

What appears to be the order of approximation of the weighted average of the mid-ordinate Euler and the improved Euler methods?

Extending the method

Consider the differential equation $\frac{dy}{dx} = -xy$.

1.   Given that the solution curve passes through $(0, 3)$, use Euler's method to find y when $x = 1$, using:

     (a)   step length, $h = 0.1$
     (b)   step length, $h = 0.05$
     (c)   step length, $h = 0.01$

In this example, the gradient function is a function of both x and y. Although the improved Euler method:

$$x_{n+1} = x_n + h; \quad y_{n+1} = y_n + h\,\frac{g(x_n, y_n) + g(x_{n+1}, y_{n+1})}{2}$$

is likely to give a more accurate solution, it does require you to know the gradient at x_1. However, you do not know y_{n+1} so you cannot use it to calculate the gradient, $g(x_{n+1}, y_{n+1})$.

A good practical solution is to use Euler's method to produce an 'interim' estimate of y_{n+1} (call this Y_{n+1}) and then use $g(x_{n+1}, Y_{n+1})$ in place of $g(x_{n+1}, y_{n+1})$.

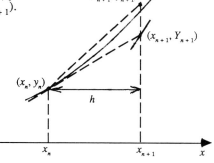

The resulting estimated point on the solution curve is:

$$x_{n+1} = x_n + h$$

$$y_{n+1} = y_n + h \times \frac{g(x_n, y_n) + g(x_{n+1}, Y_{n+1})}{2}$$

where $Y_{n+1} = y_n + hg(x_n, y_n)$

2.   Write a short program for a computer or graphic calculator which will solve a differential equation defined in terms of x and y using the improved Euler method.

3.   Repeat question 1 using the improved Euler method.

4.   (a)   Differentiate the function $y = ke^{-\frac{1}{2}x^2}$ and show that the result can be written as $\frac{dy}{dx} = -xy$.

     (b)   Explain why $y = 3e^{-\frac{1}{2}x^2}$ if the solution curve passes through $(0, 3)$.

     (c)   Hence write down the correct value of y when $x = 1$.

(continued)

5. By considering your answers to questions 1, 3 and 4(c) conjecture the order of approximation of:

   (a) the Euler method;

   (b) the improved Euler method.

6. Explain how you would solve differential equations of the type $\frac{dy}{dx} = g(x, y)$ using the mid-point Euler method.

7. Repeat questions 2, 3 and 5 for the mid-point Euler method.

Although the fourth order Runge-Kutta method can be extended to give very accurate solutions to differential equations of the type $\frac{dy}{dx} = g(x, y)$, the method is more complicated and is not simply a weighted average of the extended improved Euler and mid-point Euler methods.

Many computer software packages use versions of the fourth order Runge-Kutta method because its accuracy enables a good solution to be found with a larger step length. The other methods may require a very small step length to achieve a solution to a required degree of accuracy and you have seen in Chapter 1 how computer calculations can go wrong when small numbers are involved.

8. Plot a family of solution curves for the differential equation $\frac{dy}{dx} = -xy$ using either a graphic calculator or (preferably) a sophisticated software package on a computer.

   Where have you seen curves of this type before?

Tutorial sheet

1.　(a)　Suppose you use the mid-point Euler method to solve $\frac{dy}{dx} = 100 \cos 100x$ with $(x_0, y_0) = (0, 0)$ and so find y when $x = 1$.

This has solution $y = \sin 100x$, and so $y \approx -0.5064$ when $x = 1$.
Complete the following table, recording the values to 3 decimal places.

Step	Estimated value of y when $x = 1$	Error
1/2		
1/4		
1/10		
1/20		

　　(b)　You should find that your results do not confirm this is a second order approximation.

Explain why the method fails to produce the expected pattern in this case.

2.　(a)　The fourth order Runge-Kutta method gives an approximate solution to a differential equation. The approximation has order of accuracy 4. Explain how a fourth order approximation differs from a second order approximation.

　　(b)　When solving a differential equation, using the fourth order Runge-Kutta method with a step length of $h = 0.2$, the error is 0.0125. Calculate what the error is likely to be if the step length is reduced to $h = 0.04$.

3.　The solution to a differential equation, using the improved Euler method with a step length of $h = -0.5$, is 3.906. When the step length is reduced to $h = -0.1$ the solution is 4.002.

　　(a)　A student uses this information to calculate 4.006 as a more accurate solution. Explain how she does this.

　　(b)　If the error is in fact 0.004 when the step length is -0.1, what step length would be needed to reduce the error to 0.00001?

4.　Consider the differential equation $\frac{dy}{dx} = \frac{x}{x^2 - 4}$.

　　(a)　Use a graph plotter (if necessary) to help you sketch the graph of $\frac{dy}{dx}$ for $-4 < x < 4$ and $-4 < y < 4$. Hence draw a rough sketch of a possible solution curve over this range.

　　(b)　Explain why it would be inappropriate to use a numerical method to calculate a solution at $x = 3$, given $(x_0, y_0) = (1, 1)$.

SOLUTIONS

1 Errors

1.1 Catastrophic errors

Exercise 1

1. (a) $2.3 \left(1 \pm \frac{0.05}{2.3}\right) \times 3.4 \left(1 \pm \frac{0.05}{3.4}\right) \div 1.1 \left(1 \pm \frac{0.05}{1.1}\right)$

    $\approx \frac{2.3 \times 3.4}{1.1} \left(1 \pm \left(\frac{0.05}{2.3} + \frac{0.05}{3.4} + \frac{0.05}{1.1}\right)\right)$

    $\approx 7.1 \, (1 \pm 0.082)$

    $\approx 7.1 \pm 0.6$

    The actual maximum is 7.72 and the actual minimum is 6.55.

    (b)   If the error for each number is doubled then so is the relative error and hence the overall error. The result is therefore in the range 7.1 ± 1.2. The actual maximum is 8.4 and the actual minimum is 6.05.

2. $\dfrac{3.57 \pm 0.05 - 3.22 \pm 0.05}{5.13 \pm 0.05 - 4.87 \pm 0.05} = \dfrac{0.35 \pm 0.1}{0.26 \pm 0.1} \approx \dfrac{0.35\,(1 \pm 0.29)}{0.26\,(1 \pm 0.38)}$

    $\approx 1.35 \, (1 \pm 0.67)$

    $\approx 1.35 \pm 0.90$

    The error in the calculation is approximately ± 0.90.

3. (a)   The possible error is ± 1.

    (b)   The possible error is ± 0.001.

4. (a) $4 \times 10^{-13} \pm (5 \times 10^{-14} + 5 \times 10^{-14}) = (4 \pm 1) \times 10^{-13}$

    (b) $\dfrac{(4 \pm 1) \times 10^{-13}}{7 \times 10^{-13}} = \dfrac{4}{7} \pm \dfrac{1}{7}$

1.2 Bits and bytes

(a)	Write in denary	(i)	00001001_2	(ii)	00101100_2
(b)	Write in binary	(i)	27	(ii)	15

(a) (i) $00001001_2 = 8 + 1$
                $= 9$

    (ii) $00101100_2 = 32 + 8 + 4$
                    $= 44$

(b) (i) $27 = 16 + 8 + 2 + 1$
             $= 11011_2$

    (ii) $15 = 8 + 4 + 2 + 1$
              $= 1111_2$

> **Write in denary** (a) 101.101_2 (b) 0.01011_2

(a) $101.101_2 = 4 + 1 + \frac{1}{2} + \frac{1}{8} = 5\frac{5}{8}$

(b) $0.01011_2 = \frac{1}{4} + \frac{1}{16} + \frac{1}{32} = \frac{11}{32}$

> (a) **By using repeated doubling, show that $\frac{1}{3}$ is represented in binary as 0.010101 ...**
>
> (b) **Find the binary representation of $\frac{4}{5}$.**
>
> (c) **Find the first ten digits of the binary expansion of π.**

(a) (b)

repeated doubling	binary digit
$\frac{1}{3} \times 2 = \frac{2}{3}$	0
$\frac{2}{3} \times 2 = 1\frac{1}{3}$	1
$\frac{1}{3} \times 2 = \frac{2}{3}$	0
$\frac{2}{3} \times 2 = 1\frac{1}{3}$	1
$\frac{1}{3} \times 2 = \frac{2}{3}$	0
$\vdots$	$\vdots$

$\frac{1}{3} = 0.010101 \ldots_2$

$\frac{4}{5} \times 2 = 1\frac{3}{5}$	1
$\frac{3}{5} \times 2 = 1\frac{1}{5}$	1
$\frac{1}{5} \times 2 = \frac{2}{5}$	0
$\frac{2}{5} \times 2 = \frac{4}{5}$	0
$\frac{4}{5} \times 2 = 1\frac{3}{5}$	1
$\vdots$	$\vdots$

$\frac{4}{5} = 0.110011001100 \ldots_2$

(c) A calculator will give $\pi = 3.141592654$. In base 2, this becomes 11 + 'a binary fraction'. The fractional part, 0.14159 ... , can be converted to base 2 using repeated doubling. This is best done on a calculator using the full display of π. The first ten digits are

$$\pi = 11.00100100 \ldots_2$$

This looks as though there may be a repeating pattern, but if you continue the process you obtain

$$\pi = 11.0010010000011111101 \ldots_2$$

Irrational numbers such as π do not have a repeating pattern when represented in any base. It is interesting to note that what appeared to be a repeating pattern for π,

$$11.001001001001001 \ldots$$

is in fact the binary representation of $\frac{22}{7}$, a common approximation for π.

1.3   Floating point notation

> **(a)**   **Use a calculator to write the following numbers in exponent form to 8 significant figures.**
>
> $$100 + \sqrt{3}, \quad 1000000 + \sqrt{2}, \quad \pi^2, \quad e^{-22}.$$
>
> **(b)**   **Convert to decimal: 1.2E2, 2E–3, 5.37E5.**

(a) $100 + \sqrt{3} = 1.0173205\text{E}2$

  $1000000 + \sqrt{2} = 1.0000014\text{E}6$

  $\pi^2 = 9.8696044\text{E}0$

  $e^{-22} = 2.7894681\text{E} -10$

(b) $1.2\text{E}2 = 120$

  $2\text{E}{-}3 = 0.002$

  $5.37\text{E}5 = 537000$

> **(a)** 0.11_2 is $\frac{1}{2} + \frac{1}{4} = \frac{3}{4}$ in base ten. Check that $\frac{3}{4} \times 2^7 = 96$.
>
> **(b)**   What base ten number does $0.1011_2 \times 2^3$ represent?

(a) $\frac{3}{4} \times 2^7 = 3 \times 2^5 = 3 \times 32 = 96$

(b) $\left(\frac{1}{2} + \frac{1}{8} + \frac{1}{16}\right) \times 8 = 4 + 1 + \frac{1}{2} = 5\frac{1}{2}$

Notice that multiplying a binary number by 2^3 has the same effect as multiplying a base 10 number by 10^3 i.e. each digit is moved three places to the left. For example, $0.1011_2 \times 2^3 = 101.1_2$.

$12.5 = \frac{25}{2}$

$\qquad = \frac{25}{32} \times 16$

$\qquad = \left(\frac{16}{32} + \frac{8}{32} + \frac{1}{32}\right) \times 16$

$\qquad = \left(\frac{1}{2} + \frac{1}{4} + \frac{1}{32}\right) \times 2^4$

$\qquad = 0.11001_2 \times 2^4$

1.4 Accuracy

(a) What base ten number is stored as

| +1010000 | 10000000 | 00000000 | 00000000 | ‖ | +0000101 | ?

(b) How would the number 38 be stored?

(a) $\left(\frac{1}{2} + \frac{1}{8} + \frac{1}{256}\right) \times 2^{(1+4)} = \frac{161}{256} \times 32$

$\qquad\qquad\qquad\qquad\quad = \frac{161}{8}$

$\qquad\qquad\qquad\qquad\quad = 20\frac{1}{8}$

(b) $38 = \frac{38}{64} \times 64$

$\qquad = \left(\frac{32}{64} + \frac{4}{64} + \frac{2}{64}\right) \times 64$

$\qquad = \left(\frac{1}{2} + \frac{1}{16} + \frac{1}{32}\right) \times 2^6$

The mantissa is 0.10011_2 and the exponent is 110_2.

The number is stored as:

| + 1001100 | 00000000 | 00000000 | 000000000 | ‖ | + 0000110 |

2 Areas

2.1 Rules for estimating areas under graphs

> Estimate $\displaystyle\int_0^1 e^{-x^2}\,dx$ by each of the rules above using two strips each time.

(i)   First ordinate: $0.5\,(e^0 + e^{-0.25}) = 0.889$
(ii) Last ordinate: $0.5\,(e^{-0.25} + e^{-1}) = 0.573$
(iii) Mid-ordinate: $0.5\,(e^{-0.0625} + e^{-0.5625}) = 0.755$
(iv) Trapezium: $0.25(e^0 + e^{-0.25} + e^{-0.25} + e^{-1}) = 0.731$

> **(a)** Describe what will happen as the strip width changes for a rule which gives a third order approximation.
>
> **(b)** The first and last ordinate rules (both first order approximations) give exact answers for constant functions but not for polynomials of degree 1 or more. For what degree of polynomial do the trapezium and mid-ordinate rules stop being exact?

(a) For third order approximations, halving the strip width will (approximately) divide the error by 2^3, or 8; dividing the width by three will divide the error by approximately 3^3, or 27, and so on.

(b) The second order approximations are only exact for constant or linear functions. They stop being exact for quadratic, or second degree functions.

2.2 Simpson's rule

> Use Simpson's rule with four strips to estimate $\displaystyle\int_0^2 \cos x\,dx$.

$$\tfrac{1}{3} \times 0.5\,(\cos 0 + 4\cos 0.5 + \cos 1) + \tfrac{1}{3} \times 0.5\,(\cos 1 + 4\cos 1.5 + \cos 2) = 0.90962$$

The error is 3.25×10^{-4}, which is less than that for the mid-ordinate rule with 20 strips and less than the error for the trapezium rule with 30 strips.

> **(a)** Check that putting $n = 4$ gives the formula for four strips.
>
> **(b)** Write down the formula for Simpson's rule with eight strips.
>
> **(c)** For Simpson's rule with n strips , explain why n must be even.

(a) –

(b) The formula for 8 strips is

$$\frac{1}{3}h\,[y_0 + y_8 + 4(y_1 + y_3 + y_5 + y_7) + 2(y_2 + y_4 + y_6)]$$

(c) The formula is built-up by using pairs of strips: (y_0, y_1, y_2), (y_2, y_3, y_4), etc. The total number of strips is therefore even.

Exercise 1

1. Simpson's rule with both 8 strips and 10 strips gives 0.7782 to 4 s.f.

2. 0.3926991. 8 strips and 10 strips both give values which round off to this answer.

3. The volume is given by the area under the graph of cross-sectional area (πr^2) against h . Using Simpson's rule for the given values:

    The volume of one section $\approx \dfrac{1}{3} \times \dfrac{6}{4} \times [\pi 2^2 + \pi 2^2 + 4(\pi 1.8^2 + \pi 1.8^2) + 2 \times \pi 1.5^2]$

    Total volume $\approx 2 \times 60.3 \approx 121$ m^3.

4. (a) $\left[x^3 + 2x^2 + 3x \right]_1^2 = 16$

    (b) Simpson's rule gives the exact answer.

5. For cubic functions, you should always obtain the exact answer using Simpson's rule with any number of strips.

6E. It is not possible to use a Simpson's rule program to integrate from $-\infty$ to $+\infty$.

    In view of the symmetry of the curve, integrating from 0 to n for different values of n brings out the properties of the curve.

    Some values obtained from a programmable calculator using Simpson's rule with 20 strips are as follows.

    The integral from 0 to 3 is 0.49865, from 0 to 4 is 0.499968 and from 0 to 5 is 0.4999997. For the integral from 0 to 7 the calculator gives 0.5 and so the area from -7 to 7 is 1.

2.3   Simpson's rule and cubic functions

> **Find the equation of this straight line approximation to $y = x^3$.**

The line goes through the points $(-h, -h^3)$, $(0, 0)$ and (h, h^3). Its gradient is h^2 and its equation is therefore $y = h^2x$.

> **Simpson's rule is a fourth order approximation. For what degree of polynomial is it exact? What appears to be the connection between the order of approximation and the degree of polynomial for which a rule is exact?**

Simpson's rule is exact for constant, linear, quadratic and cubic functions. It appears that the order of approximation of a rule is one more than the highest degree of polynomial for which the rule is always exact.

3 Taylor polynomials

3.1 Quadratic approximations

> **(a)** In the example, explain why $h = x - 2$ and hence why
> $$x^{-1} \approx \frac{1}{2} - \frac{(x-2)}{4}$$
>
> **(b)** Use a graph plotter to superimpose the graphs of $y = x^{-1}$
> and $y = \frac{1}{2} - \frac{(x-2)}{4}$ for $1.5 < x < 2.5$ and $0.4 < y < 0.6$.

(a) h is the horizontal displacement from $x = 2$ and so $h = x - 2$.

Then $x^{-1} \approx \frac{1}{2} - \frac{h}{4}$

$\approx \frac{1}{2} - \frac{x-2}{4}$

(b) The graphs are very similar!

3.2 Estimating gradients numerically

> Use formula ① to estimate the gradient of the graph of $2^{\cos x}$ at the point
> where $x = 1$. Write down the answers you get for $h = 0.1, 0.01, 0.001$ and so
> on until you are sure that you have the answer correct to 4 s.f.

$h = 10^{-4}$ and $h = 10^{-5}$ both give -0.8482 (4 s.f.)

> Show that this formula rearranges to give:
> $$f'(a) \approx \frac{f(a+h) - f(a-h)}{2h}$$

$$f(a+h) - f(a-h) \approx f(a) + f'(a)h + f''(a)\frac{h^2}{2} - \left(f(a) - f'(a)h + f''(a)\frac{h^2}{2} \right)$$

$$\approx 2f'(a)h$$

$$\text{So } f'(a) \approx \frac{f(a+h) - f(a-h)}{2h}$$

> Use formula ② to estimate the gradient of the graph of $2^{\cos x}$ at the
> point where $x = 1$, using $h = 0.1, 0.01$ and so on. Compare your
> answers with those obtained by using formula ①.

$h = 0.01$ and $h = 0.001$ both give -0.8482 (4 s.f.)

Formula ② gives an answer to 4 significant figures for a smaller value of h.

(a) Copy and complete the table below:

Errors when using formula ①

	h = 0.01	h = 0.002	h = 0.001
$y = \sin x$ at $x = 2$	0.00454		
$y = \sin x$ at $x = 1$			
$y = e^x$ at $x = 1$			

(b) What happens to the error when the value of h is divided by 5 and when it is divided by 10?

(c) What does the order of accuracy of this method appear to be?

(d) Complete another table, similar to the one shown above, using formula ② .

(e) What does the order of accuracy of this method appear to be?

(a)

	$h = 0.01$	$h = 0.002$	$h = 0.001$
$\sin x$ at $x = 2$	0.00454	0.000909	0.000455
$\sin x$ at $x = 1$	0.00422	0.000842	0.000421
e^x at $x = 1$	0.0136	0.00272	0.00136

(b) When h is divided by 5 the error is (approximately) divided by 5.
When h is divided by 10 the error is (approximately) divided by 10.

(c) First order.

(d)

	$h = 0.01$	$h = 0.002$	$h = 0.001$
$\sin x$ at $x = 2$	6.94×10^{-6}	2.77×10^{-7}	6.94×10^{-8}
$\sin x$ at $x = 1$	9.00×10^{-6}	3.60×10^{-7}	9.01×10^{-8}
e^x at $x = 1$	4.53×10^{-5}	1.81×10^{-6}	4.53×10^{-7}

(e) Second order.

3.3 Higher degree Taylor polynomials

What is Taylor's second approximation to $f(x) = e^x$ centred on $x = 0$?

$$f(x) = e^x \Rightarrow f(0) = f'(0) = f''(0) = 1$$

$$e^x \approx 1 + x + \frac{x^2}{2!}$$

(a) Work out $f''(0)$ and $f^{(3)}(0)$ and so find expressions for r and s.

(b) Explain how the answers above give, for Taylor's third approximation:

$$f(x) \approx f(0) + f'(0)x + f''(0)\,\frac{x^2}{2!} + f^{(3)}(0)\,\frac{x^3}{3!}$$

(c) Write down Taylor's third approximation to $f(x) = e^x$ centred on $x = 0$.

(a) $f''(0) = 2r \Rightarrow r = \frac{1}{2}f''(0)$ or $\frac{1}{2!}f''(0)$

$f^{(3)}(0) = 3 \times 2s \Rightarrow s = \frac{1}{6}f^{(3)}(0)$ or $\frac{1}{3!}f^{(3)}(0)$

(b) Substituting the above into $g(x) = p + qx + rx^2 + sx^3$ gives

$$g(x) = f(0) + f'(0)x + f''(0)\,\frac{x^2}{2!} + f^{(3)}(0)\,\frac{x^3}{3!} \text{ and } f(x) \approx g(x)$$

(c) $e^x \approx 1 + x + \dfrac{x^2}{2!} + \dfrac{x^3}{3!}$

(a) Work out Taylor's fourth approximation by starting with:

$$f(x) \approx g(x) \text{ where } g(x) = p + qx + rx^2 + sx^3 + tx^4$$

(b) Write down Taylor's fifth approximation centred on $x = 0$.

(c) Write down Taylor's fifth approximation to $f(x) = e^x$ centred on $x = 0$.

(a) $f(0) = p \qquad f'(0) = q \qquad f''(0) = 2r \qquad f^{(3)}(0) = 3 \times 2s$

$f^{(4)}(0) = 4 \times 3 \times 2t$

So $f(x) \approx f(0) + f'(0)x + f''(0)\,\dfrac{x^2}{2!} + f^{(3)}(0)\,\dfrac{x^3}{3!} + f^{(4)}(0)\,\dfrac{x^4}{4!}$

(b) $f(x) \approx f(0) + f'(0)x + f''(0)\,\dfrac{x^2}{2!} + f^{(3)}(0)\,\dfrac{x^3}{3!} + f^{(4)}(0)\,\dfrac{x^4}{4!} + f^{(5)}(0)\,\dfrac{x^5}{5!}$

(c) $e^x \approx 1 + x + \dfrac{x^2}{2!} + \dfrac{x^3}{3!} + \dfrac{x^4}{4!} + \dfrac{x^5}{5!}$

> **Show that Taylor's seventh approximation to f(x) = sin x centred on $x = 0$ is**
> $$\sin x \approx x - \frac{x^3}{3!} + \frac{x^5}{5!} - \frac{x^7}{7!}$$

f(x)	= sin x	$\Rightarrow$ f(0)	= 0
f$'(x)$	= cos x	$\Rightarrow$ f$'(0)$	= 1
f$''(x)$	= $-$ sin x	$\Rightarrow$ f$''(0)$	= 0
f$^{(3)}(x)$	= $-$ cos x	$\Rightarrow$ f$^{(3)}(0)$	= -1
f$^{(4)}(x)$	= sin x	$\Rightarrow$ f$^{(4)}(0)$	= 0
f$^{(5)}(x)$	= cos x	$\Rightarrow$ f$^{(5)}(0)$	= 1
f$^{(6)}(x)$	= $-$ sin x	$\Rightarrow$ f$^{(6)}(0)$	= 0
f$^{(7)}(x)$	= $-$ cos x	$\Rightarrow$ f$^{(7)}(0)$	= -1

Therefore $\sin x \approx x - \dfrac{x^3}{3!} + \dfrac{x^5}{5!} - \dfrac{x^7}{7!}$

Exercise 1

1. (a) $1 + nx + \dfrac{n(n-1)}{2!}x^2 + \dfrac{n(n-1)(n-2)}{3!}x^3 + \dfrac{n(n-1)(n-2)(n-3)}{4!}x^4$

   (b) $1 - x + \dfrac{(-1)(-2)}{2!}x^2 + \dfrac{(-1)(-2)(-3)}{3!}x^3 + \dfrac{(-1)(-2)(-3)(-4)}{4!}x^4$

   $= 1 - x + x^2 - x^3 + x^4$

   (c) $1 - (-x) + (-x)^2 - (-x)^3 + (-x)^4 = 1 + x + x^2 + x^3 + x^4$

   (d) $a = 1$ and $r = x$, so $s_\infty = \dfrac{1}{1-x}$.

   $\dfrac{1}{1-x} = (1-x)^{-1}$ and so the G.P. result agrees with the Taylor approximation.

   $1 - x + x^2 - x^3 + \ldots = \dfrac{1}{1-(-x)} = \dfrac{1}{1+x}$. This agrees with the Taylor approximation for $(1 + x)^{-1}$.

2. $(1+x)^{\frac{1}{2}} \approx 1 + \dfrac{1}{2}x - \dfrac{1}{8}x^2 + \dfrac{1}{16}x^3 - \dfrac{5}{128}x^4 + \dfrac{7}{256}x^5$

   $(1 + 0.21)^{\frac{1}{2}} = 1.1$, whereas the Taylor approximation gives 1.1000015 (7 d.p.).

3. (a) $\sin 2x \approx 2x - \dfrac{(2x)^3}{3!} + \dfrac{(2x)^5}{5!} \approx 2x - \dfrac{4}{3}x^3 + \dfrac{4}{15}x^5$

   (b) $\sin 0.5\,x \approx 0.5x - \dfrac{(0.5x)^3}{3!} + \dfrac{(0.5x)^5}{5!} \approx 0.5x - \dfrac{1}{48}x^3 + \dfrac{1}{3840}x^5$

4. (a) If $f(x) = \ln x$, both $f(0)$ and $f'(0)$ are undefined.

   (b) If $f(x) = \ln(1+x)$, $f(0)$, $f'(0)$, $f''(0)$, ... can all be evaluated.

$$f(x) = \ln(1+x) \Rightarrow f(0) = \ln 1 = 0$$
$$f'(x) = \frac{1}{1+x} \Rightarrow f'(0) = 1$$
$$f''(x) = -\frac{1}{(1+x)^2} \Rightarrow f''(0) = -1$$

So $\ln(1+x) \approx 0 + x - \frac{x^2}{2!} = x - \frac{x^2}{2}$

   (c) $\ln(1 + 0.2x) \approx 0.2x - \frac{(0.2x)^2}{2!}$

$$\approx 0.2x - 0.02x^2$$

3.4 Radius of convergence

> Write a short program for a graphic calculator or a computer to calculate and display S_r for values of r increasing in steps of 1 from $r = 0$ when $x = 0.6$. For what value of r does Taylor's rth approximation give an accurate value when rounded to 4 decimal places?

A program is given in the unit guide.

When $r = 21$, the answer is correct to 4 decimal places.

> (a) For which values of x does Taylor's approximation appear to converge on the correct value of the function?
>
> (b) Explain why the approximation is of no use for $|x| \geq 1$.

(a) The approximation appears to converge for $-1 < x < 1$.

(b) For $|x| \geq 1$, successive terms of the series do not become smaller. (For $|x| > 1$ they become larger.)

Exercise 2

1. (a) $\ln(1+x) = x - \frac{x^2}{2} + \frac{x^3}{3} - \frac{x^4}{4} + \dots$

   (b) $\ln(1 + 0.4x) = 0.4x - 0.16\frac{x^2}{2} + 0.064\frac{x^3}{3} - 0.0256\frac{x^4}{4}.$

   (c) $-1 < 0.4x \leq 1 \Rightarrow -2.5 < x \leq 2.5$

2. (a) $\sin x = x - \dfrac{x^3}{3!} + \dfrac{x^5}{5!} - \dfrac{x^7}{7!} + \dots$

(b) $\sin 2x = 2x - \dfrac{8x^3}{3!} + \dfrac{32x^5}{5!} - \dfrac{128x^7}{7!} + \dots$

(c) Valid for all x.

(d) The graphs agree approximately on the range $-2 < x < 2$. As higher degree polynomials are considered, the range of x for which the approximation is good becomes larger.

3E. (a) $3\left(\dfrac{1}{1 + 0.5x}\right)$

(b) $3(1 - 0.5x + (0.5x)^2 + \dots \ )$

(c) $-1 < 0.5x < 1 \implies -2 < x < 2$.

3.5   Order of accuracy

(a) What happens when you double the value of x in the first, second, third and fourth approximations?

(b) What happens when you treble the value of x?

(c) How does the degree of the approximation appear to be connected to the order of accuracy?

(d) Produce a similar table for the function e^x for $r = 1$ and 2. Check the conjecture you made in (c).

(a) When you double x,

First approximation   – The error is multiplied by 2^2 (approximately).
Second approximation – The error is multiplied by 2^3 (approximately).
Third approximation   – The error is multiplied by 2^4 (approximately).
Fourth approximation – The error is multiplied by 2^5 (approximately).

(b) When you treble x,

First approximation   – The error is multiplied by 3^2 (approximately).
Second approximation – The error is multiplied by 3^3 (approximately).
Third approximation   – The error is multiplied by 3^4 (approximately).
Fourth approximation – The error is multiplied by 3^5 (approximately).

(c) The order of accuracy appears to be one more than the degree of the approximation.

(d) $e^x \approx 1 + x + \dfrac{x^2}{2!}$

	$x = 0.01$	$x = 0.02$	$x = 0.03$
$r = 1$	5.02×10^{-5}	20.1×10^{-5}	45.5×10^{-5}
$r = 2$	1.67×10^{-7}	13.4×10^{-7}	45.3×10^{-7}

(a) How does the work above explain why Taylor's first approximation has second order accuracy?

(b) For Taylor's second approximation, what power of x will the first term of the error series contain? How does this explain the order of accuracy of Taylor's second approximation?

(c) Explain how similar reasoning will lead to the fact the the order of accuracy of a Taylor polynomial is always one more than the degree of the approximation, provided x is small.

(a) Most of the error will be contained in a term of the form ax^2 (where a is a constant). When x is multiplied by any number, r, the error will become approximately $a(xr)^2$ and so will be multiplied by r^2. The approximation therefore has second order accuracy.

(b) The first term in the error series will be the x^3 term. This term will be multiplied by r^3 when x is multiplied by r, so the error will be approximately multiplied by r^3.

(c) The first term of the error series will generally contribute most of the error. For a Taylor polynomial of degree n, the first error term will be the x^{n+1} term and so the order of accuracy will be $n + 1$.

4 *Solving equations*

4.1 Chaos

> If the initial population $p_0 = 0.2$ and the boom factor $k = 3.2$, use May's population model to calculate the population figures for the next ten years.

The population figures, correct to 3 decimal places, are:

$p_1 = 0.512$ $p_2 = 0.800$ $p_3 = 0.513$ $p_4 = 0.799$ $p_5 = 0.513$

$p_6 = 0.799$ $p_7 = 0.513$ $p_8 = 0.799$ $p_9 = 0.513$ $p_{10} = 0.799$

The fish population appears to oscillate between two states. If you try a different initial population, you will obtain a similar result, but it may take longer to settle down to a stable pattern.

> Write a short program for a computer or a graphic calculator to calculate and illustrate how population figures fluctuate according to May's model. (Help for this is given in the unit guide.)
>
> (a)   Investigate the iteration $p_{n+1} = kp_n (1 - p_n)$, where $p_0 = 0.2$ and k takes the following values:
>
> (i) $k = 0.5$ (ii) $k = 1$ (iii) $k = 2$ (iv) $k = 3$
>
> (v) $k = 3.2$ (vi) $k = 3.5$ (vii) $k = 3.6$ (viii) $k = 4$
>
> (b)   Comment on what you find.

(a,b) (i)   The population approaches zero (i.e. becomes extinct).

(ii)   The population approaches zero (i.e. becomes extinct).

(iii) The population rapidly approaches 0.5 and remains stable at this value.

(iv)   The population appears to oscillate between two values. However, these values are not stable and are both approaching 0.66666 ... **very** slowly. It would take many millions of iterations for this stable value to be reached to the accuracy displayed on the calculator.

(v)   The population settles down after a while to oscillate between two values, $p = 0.51304 \ldots$ and $p = 0.79945 \ldots$

(vi) The population settles down to a steady cycle of four values. It goes from $p = 0.50088 \ldots$ to $p = 0.87499 \ldots$ to $p = 0.38281 \ldots$ to $p = 0.82694 \ldots$ and back to $p = 0.50088 \ldots$ to repeat the cycle.

(vii) The population does not settle down to a predictable pattern. It appears to fluctuate in a chaotic manner, but always within two ranges, approximately $0.3 < p < 0.6$ and $0.79 < p < 0.9$ and always oscillating from one to the other.

(viii) The population does not settle down. It appears to fluctuate in a chaotic manner assuming any value between 0 and 1 in a seemingly random way.

4.2   Bisection and decimal search

> **The equation $\sin x + e^{x-5} = 0$ is known to have a root between $x = 3$ and $x = 4$. Suppose you use decimal search and find the root is in the interval $3.331 \rightarrow 3.332$.**
>
> **(a)   How many function calculations would you have done?**
>
> **(b)   If a root is known to lie between two consecutive integers, what are the maximum and the minimum number of function calculations needed to narrow the interval down to the third decimal place?**
>
> **(c)   About how many function calculations would be needed 'on average' to narrow the interval down to the third decimal place using decimal search?**

(a) You would need 4 calculations to locate the first decimal place, 4 for the second and 2 for the third. You would therefore need 10 function calculations altogether.

(b) You need at least 1 function calculation (you might need as many as 9) to locate each decimal place. To narrow an interval down to the third decimal place would require a maximum of 27 and a minimum of 3 calculations

(c) As you need between 3 and 27 calculations, you might expect to need 15 'on average'. In actual fact, assuming that all ten digits are equally likely to appear in any of the first three decimal places of a root, a probability function for the number of function calculations needed can be deduced and the mean number calculated. If you do this for just one decimal place you obtain:

No. of calculations	1	2	3	4	5	6	7	8	9
Probability	0.1	0.1	0.1	0.1	0.1	0.1	0.1	0.1	0.2

This gives a mean number of 5.4 calculations per decimal place. You would therefore expect to need 16.2 calculations for three decimal places.

(a) **If the interval from $x = a$ to $x = b$ is bisected n times, what is the length of the resulting sub-interval?**

(b) **You can use bisection to solve the equation $\sin x + e^{x-5} = 0$. Knowing that there is a root between $x = 3$ and $x = 4$, how many function calculations are necessary to reduce the interval length to 0.001?**

(c) **Which algorithm do you think is the more efficient; decimal search or bisection?**

(a) Each repeated application of the bisection method captures the root in an interval half the size of what it was. The size of the interval after n applications is therefore the original size, $b - a$, divided by 2^n.

(b) $\dfrac{4-3}{2^{10}}$ is approximately 0.001 so 10 function calculations would be needed.

(c) Both algorithms achieve the same degree of accuracy after 10 function calculations in the particular example looked at. In general, however, you would expect bisection to be slightly more efficient, as only 10 function calculations are needed to achieve three decimal places accuracy, whereas 16.2 are needed, on average, using decimal search.

4.3 Iteration

Write a short program for a computer or a graphic calculator to generate and continue this sequence until you can state the solution to the equation correct to 3 decimal places.

Below are two sample programs, one in BASIC, the other for a Casio graphic calculator

BASIC

```
10  INPUT X
20  LET X = COS(X)
30  PRINT X
40  GOTO 20
```

fx–7000G

```
? → X
Lbl 1
cos X → X◢
Goto 1
```

(a)   Sketch the graphs of $y = x$ and $y = \cos x$ on the same axes in the range $0.4 < x < 1.1$ and $0.4 < y < 1.1$.

(b)   Show the two stages in the iteration which takes $x_0 = 1$ to $x_1 = 0.540$.

(c)   On the same diagram, show the stages from:

$x_1 = 0.540$ to $x_2 = 0.858$
$x_2 = 0.858$ to $x_3 = 0.654$
$x_3 = 0.654$ to $x_4 = 0.793$
etc ...

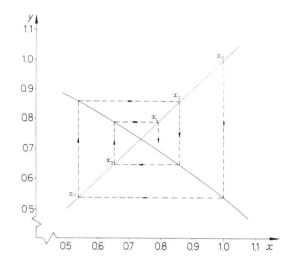

Under what conditions will iteration be a more efficient method of locating a root than bisection?

If the starting value is near the root, where the graph is locally straight, and $g'(a) = \frac{1}{2}$, each successive iteration will halve the error. In this case, iteration will be just as efficient as bisection.

Iteration will be more efficient than bisection if $g'(a) < \frac{1}{2}$. The fact that iteration is an easy process to program is of considerable practical importance and can outweigh considerations of efficiency.

Exercise 1

1. (a) $(2x - 3)(2x - 3) = 0 \Rightarrow x = 1.5$

   (b) Solve by iteration.

   (c) The sequence converges to $x = 1.5$ when the start value, x_0, is in the range $1.5 < x_0 < 3.5$. When $x_0 = 3.5$, $x_1 = x_2 = \ldots = 1.5$.

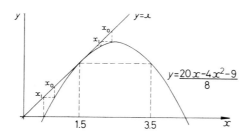

   (d) $g(x) = \dfrac{20x - 4x^2 - 9}{8} \Rightarrow g'(x) = \dfrac{20 - 8x}{8}$

   Iteration gets slower and slower as $x_n \to 1.5$ because $g'(1.5) = 1$.

2. (a) For any start value, x_0, (other than $x = 0$ or $x = 1$) the iteration oscillates between the start value and $1 \div x_0$.

   (b) The function is self-inverse (i.e. $g^{-1}(x) = \dfrac{1}{x}$).

   (c) For any self-inverse function, $g(x)$,

   $$x_1 = g(x_0) \Rightarrow x_0 = g(x_1)$$

   but $x_2 = g(x_1)$, therefore $x_2 = x_0$

   so the iterative sequence becomes $x_0, x_1, x_0, x_1, x_0, x_1 \ldots$

3. (a) $x_{n+1} = 500 + 0.6x_n + 0.3x_n$
          $= 500 + 0.9x_n$

   (b) (i) $x_5 = 2638$ (ii) $x_{10} = 3605$ (iii) $x_{100} = 5000$

   (c) (i) $x_5 = 6771$ (ii) $x_{10} = 6046$ (iii) $x_{100} = 5000$

   The fish population will eventually reach a stable number of 5000, regardless of how many there are to start with. This is the solution to the equation $x = 500 + 0.9x$.

4.4   The Newton-Raphson method

> Explain why $f'(a) = \dfrac{f(a)}{a-b}$ and hence show that $b = a - \dfrac{f(a)}{f'(a)}$.

$$f'(a) = \frac{\text{change in } y \text{ along tangent}}{\text{change in } x \text{ along tangent}}$$

$$= \frac{f(a)}{a-b}$$

$$f'(a) = \frac{f(a)}{a-b} \implies a-b = \frac{f(a)}{f'(a)} \implies b = a - \frac{f(a)}{f'(a)}$$

> (a)   Solve the equation $x - \cos x = 0$ using the Newton-Raphson process starting at $x = 1$.
>
> (b)   Compare this method with an $x_{n+1} = \cos x_n$ iteration.

(a)   If $a = 1$ then $b = 1 - \dfrac{(1 - \cos 1)}{(1 + \sin 1)} = 0.7504$ (4 d.p.)

If $a = 0.7504$ then $b = 0.7391$ (4 d.p.)

If $a = 0.7391$ then $b = 0.7391$ (4 d.p.)

As the value of the estimate is unchanged at four decimal places, the root of the equation must be $x = 0.739$ (3 d.p.).

(b)   It takes over 20 iterations to achieve a similar degree of accuracy (i.e. 0.7391) to that achieved after 3 iterations using the Newton-Raphson method.

> Use a software package such as *The Newton-Raphson method* in *Numerical solutions to equations* to solve the equation $x - \cos x = 0$ starting at
>
> (a) $x = 1$ (b) $x = 3$ (c) $x = 4.5$

(a)   The sequence converges on the zero very quickly and gives a solution to 4 decimal places after just 3 iterations.

(b)   The sequence oscillates slightly then converges on the zero very quickly and gives a solution to 6 decimal places after just 6 iterations.

(c)   The sequence jumps about unpredictably without finding the zero. This chaotic behaviour is a good example of what can happen if the starting value is near a turning point.

If $\quad x_{n+1} = x_n - \dfrac{f(x_n)}{f'(x_n)} \quad$ and $f'(x_n) \approx \dfrac{f(x_n + h) - f(x_n)}{h}$

then $x_{n+1} \approx x_n - f(x_n) \div \dfrac{f(x_n + h) - f(x_n)}{h}$

$\qquad\qquad \approx x_n - \dfrac{h\,f(x_n)}{f(x_n + h) - f(x_n)}$

Exercise 2

1. (a) The zeros are 0.2907 ... , 2.8060 ... and 4.9032 ...

    (b) (i)   2.8060 ...   (ii)   0.2907 ...

         (iii) 4.9032 ...   (iv)   0.2907 ...

    (c) Starting values in this range bring you near a turning point and the method
         becomes unpredictable.

         For example, a first order numerical method gives the following results
         in cases (ii) and (iii).

         (ii)   Starting at 3.75, the zero 0.2907 is obtained for $h = 0.1$ and
                 $h = 0.001$, whereas 4.9032 is obtained for $h = 0.01, 0.05$ and 0.08.

         (iii)   Starting at 3.77, the zero 0.2907 is obtained for $h = 0.1$, whereas
                 4.9032 is obtained for $h = 0.01$ and 0.001.

5 Differential equations

5.2 Improving accuracy

> For each of the two improved methods, complete a table of errors similar to the one completed for Euler's method in the previous section (use the same differential equation).
>
> What appears to be the order of approximation of:
>
> (a)   the mid-point Euler method;
>
> (b)   the improved Euler method?
>
> Which method do you prefer and why?

Mid-point Euler

	Step	Estimated value of y when $x = 2$	Error
	1/2	7.9375	0.0625
$\div 2$	1/4	7.98438	0.01563
	1/8	7.996094	0.003906 $\div 2^2$
	1/16	7.9990234	0.0009766
$\div 10$	1/20	7.999375	0.000625 $\div 10^2$

Improved Euler

	Step	Estimated value of y when $x = 2$	Error
	1/2	8.125	0.125
$\div 2$	1/4	8.03125	0.03125
	1/8	8.007813	0.007813 $\div 2^2$
	1/16	8.001953	0.001953
$\div 10$	1/20	8.00125	0.00125 $\div 10^2$

(a)(b)   In each case, dividing the step length by a factor λ causes the error to be divided by λ^2. Both methods are second order approximations. The mid-point method is preferred because it is more accurate. The error of the mid-point method is consistently half that of the improved Euler method for this differential equation.

> **You may wonder if it is appropriate to quote a five significant figure value for *y*. How accurate do you think this answer is?**
>
> **If you run a computer program with 1500 steps of 0.001 to solve this problem, then you will probably feel confident that your result is accurate. Do this and see how accurate an answer $y = 0.77826$ really is.**

The mid-point Euler method gives $y = 0.77824$ (5 d.p.). If you use numbers rounded to 5 decimal places in your calculations, you would expect the fifth decimal place of your answer to be unreliable and so a difference of only 0.00002 between the two results shows remarkable agreement, especially since the step lengths used in Example 1 are not particularly small.

Exercise 1

1. $y - 0.73896 = 4(y - 0.76841)$
   $\Rightarrow y \approx 0.7782$

2.

Step	Error
0.2	0.085
0.1	0.043

The error is halved when the step is halved. On this evidence, the method would appear to be a first order approximation and so the calculator probably uses Euler's method.

5.3   Fourth order Runge-Kutta

> **Use the fourth order Runge-Kutta method with a negative step to estimate *s* to 4 decimal places when $t = -2$.**

Step	Estimated value of s when $t = -2$
-1	2.11819
$-1/2$	2.11793
$-1/4$	2.11792
$-1/8$	2.11792

The estimate does not change in the fifth decimal place when the step is halved from $-\frac{1}{4}$ to $-\frac{1}{8}$. You can therefore be confident about rounding the result to 4 decimal places.

$s \approx 2.1179$ when $t = -2$

Exercise 2

1. Fourth order Runge-Kutta $= \dfrac{2 \times \text{Mid-point Euler} + \text{Improved Euler}}{3}$

    $\phantom{\text{Fourth order Runge-Kutta }} = \dfrac{2 \times 0.74874713 + 0.74298410}{3}$

    $\phantom{\text{Fourth order Runge-Kutta }} = 0.74682612$

2. (a) If the correct value is y, then the error is $y - 1.416653583$ when the step length is 1 and the error is $y - 1.416152927$ when the step length is $\frac{1}{3}$. If the method is a fourth order approximation, then dividing the step length by 3 would divide the error by $3^4 = 81$.

    So $81(y - 1.416152927) = y - 1.416653583 \Rightarrow y = 1.416146669$

    (b) $\frac{dy}{dx} = \sin x \Rightarrow y = -\cos x + c$

    $y = 0$ when $x = 0$ and so $y = -\cos x + 1$

    When $x = 2$, $y = -\cos 2 + 1 = 1.416146837$

    The answer to (a) is not precise because the Runge-Kutta method is a fourth order approximation for small step lengths. For this function, step lengths of 1 and $\frac{1}{3}$ are **not** sufficiently small.

3. As this is a fourth order approximation, dividing the step length by 10 should result in the error being divided by 10 000. Thus, if the error in the second approximation is e then the difference betwen the two estimates is 9999e.

So $9999e = 0.778237903 - 0.778237804$

$\Rightarrow e \approx 1 \times 10^{-11}$

It is very unlikely that this error will affect the ninth decimal place and so it is reasonable to take the second result as being accurate to nine decimal places.

5.4 Extending the method

> Write down a recurrence relation for solving $\frac{dy}{dx} = \cos x$ based on:
>
> (a)   Taylor's second approximation;
>
> (b)   Taylor's third approximation.

$$g(x) = \cos x \implies g'(x) = -\sin x$$
$$\implies g''(x) = -\cos x$$

(a) $y_{n+1} = y_n + h \cos x_n - \dfrac{h^2}{2} \sin x_n$

      $x_{n+1} = x_n + h$

(b) $y_{n+1} = y_n + h \cos x_n - \dfrac{h^2}{2} \sin x_n - \dfrac{h^3}{6} \cos x_n$

      $x_{n+1} = x_n + h$

5.5 Avoiding disaster

> What happens if you try to use the improved Euler method with $(x_0, y_0) = (-1, 1)$ to solve the differential equation $\frac{dy}{dx} = -\frac{1}{x^2}$ for $x = 2$ using:
>
> (a)   step length $h = 0.3$;
>
> (b)   step length $h = 0.2$?
>
> Explain why the method fails.

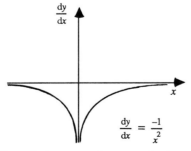

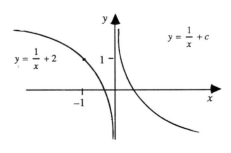

The solution curve has a vertical asymptote when $x = 0$. When the step length is 0.3, the method 'jumps' over this asymptote in an unpredictable way. When the step length is 0.2 the method fails because you cannot divide by zero.

The solution curve passes through $(-1, 1)$ and so $y = \dfrac{1}{x} + 2$ for $x < 0$. For $x > 0$, $y = \dfrac{1}{x} + c$, where c can only be determined if there is a known point for $x > 0$.